American Gun Culture
Collectors, Shows and the Story of the Gun
Second Edition

American Gun Culture
Collectors, Shows and the Story of the Gun
Second Edition

Jimmy D. Taylor

LFB Scholarly Publishing LLC
El Paso 2014

Library of Congress Cataloging-in-Publication Data

Taylor, Jimmy D., 1973-
    American gun culture : collectors, shows, and the story of the gun /
Jimmy D. Taylor.
        pages cm
    Includes bibliographical references and index.
    ISBN 978-1-59332-621-0 (pbk. : alk. paper)
    1. Firearms--Social aspects--United States. 2. Firearms ownership--
United States--History. 3. Firearms--United States--Collectors and
collecting. I. Title. II. Series: Criminal justice (LFB Scholarly
Publishing LLC)
    TS533.2.T39 2014
    683.4--dc23
                                        2013033966

ISBN 978-1-59332-621-0 - Second Edition

Printed on acid-free 250-year-life paper.

Manufactured in the United States of America.

In loving memory of Graham Martin...

Table of Contents

List of Charts and Tables

Tables

Charts

List of Images

Preface

From previous books and research efforts, as well as the general findings of Taylor (2009), we know that there are a lot of guns in the United States of America. Guns are all around us. Not only is there a very real physical presence of guns in the United States, their symbolism permeates American culture in other ways, ranging from heated political debates and landmark court cases to popular trade publications, song references, television shows, movies, and even t-shirt slogans. But what do all of these guns really mean to their owners? This is an important area of gun ownership that has been overlooked by researchers and policy makers alike. This book explores the culturally-based symbolic meaning of guns, and the ways in which the meaning of gun ownership, as well as the symbolic meaning imbued in individual guns influences aspects of gun ownership, gun use, and even everyday social interaction.

This ethnographic research effort applies an experimental mix of thick, descriptive methods of observation and grounded theoretical techniques to this largely unexplored aspect of U.S. gun culture. A total of 52 interviews of varying length were conducted with a range of gun owners in venues that included gun collectors' homes, shooting events, and public gun shows in the Midwest. Subjects were asked to share the stories of their guns, and explore the value and meaning of separate guns in their collections. The interviews were supplemented with follow-up conversations with most of the original respondents, and an additional twenty three gun-collecting informants. Additionally, content analysis was conducted on a variety of gun-related popular media (i.e. gun violence in the news, TV shows, movies, songs, magazines and trade publications).

Some interesting findings are revealed, which are not limited to the following: 1) Guns, as an aspect of culture, or product of social interaction, are rich with symbolic values; 2) For many gun owners, the value placed on guns is far more emotional in nature than monetary (i.e. In addition to their intended functions as security implements, instruments of death, recreational sporting goods and even collectible artifacts, guns also frequently serve as a type of emotional conduit with healthy, "non-toxic" consequences); 3) The value assigned to guns by their owners appears to influence the way in which gun owners interact with their guns as well as their social audience; 4) Gun owners recognize a unique type of stigma associated with these cultural products, and respond through a complex series of stigma management techniques; and 5) U.S. gun culture involves a series of deference and demeanor-filled rituals; rituals pertaining to being the gun owner, the gun user, and possibly even the gun as an object of near-worship.

It is worth noting that the sensitivity to stigma among gun owners is common enough and strong enough to consider for social policy. The preliminary findings of this study suggest that gun owners would be very receptive to initiatives as simple as public service announcements and media coverage admonishing (or stigmatizing) those who use or store firearms incorrectly. Safety and appropriate use are highly-important to gun advocacy groups. This is evidenced not only in literature common at gun shows and among various pro-gun organizations, but also through the educational and training services proactively supported by them. This is one area where there is great potential for both pro and anti-gun groups to agree on something: stigmatize the misuse of guns and you will save lives. By stigmatizing the misuse of guns (instead of gun ownership itself), policy makers and political action groups avoid the pitfalls, delays and countless debates over issues such as treading on the liberties of others. Another advantage is that such initiatives would be relatively quick and cost-effective, as well.

Acknowledgements

I am grateful to my family and friends for their continued support throughout this process.

This list is far from complete, but I must first thank Leo Balk of LFB Scholarly Publishing, for the interest in my manuscript, and active support throughout the editing process. Your encouragement, generosity and support of scholarly writing is a notable contribution to the scientific community.

I am also grateful for the insightful advice and patience of my friend and long-time mentor and adviser, Martin D. Schwartz. Marty, you have given me sound advice for close to two decades, and I hope to work with you for many years to come. To my original project supervisor, Dr. Tim Curry, whose unobtrusive help and rare ability to help a researcher tease out interesting observations from a mountain of data proved invaluable, I thank you. I started with a seemingly simple research question that turned into a multi-headed monster. Your approach to scholarship made the monster a little less frightening. Any scholar is privileged to work under you.

To Keith Haley, I would like to say thank you for your continued support, loyalty and contagious enthusiasm. I am also grateful for the suggestions and receptive ears of Paul Bellair and Steven Lopez, Leon Anderson for dedicating so much time and energy to providing feedback on my research and helping me to narrow my focus and consider avenues that I would otherwise have not, the much-needed guidance of my friends and colleagues, Charles Savage, Ed Rhine, Jimmy D. Weaver, Ron Raines, Tom Roth, and Ramblin' Don Rhodes. Editorial Assistants, Robin Akamik and Amanda Lanning, your help was vital. And certainly not last by any stretch of the imagination, the openness and willingness of my many gun-owning informants.

Finally, I would surely never have survived even the first draft of a single chapter without the love of my wife Katie Taylor, the non-stop amusement of my children Graham, Charlie and Lily, or the lifetime of encouragement from my parents Toni and Ronney Talley and Charles and Arlyene Taylor. Without each of you, there would be no acknowledgements page, as I never would have finished writing any books.

CHAPTER I

Introduction: The Guns Among Us

There was a kid named Gene who lived up the hill from me, on the same street where I grew up. About Gene, I can say this: I was never entirely sure that I liked him, but we rode bikes together on many an after school adventure. He was older, cooler and popular with the girls on the bus and in the neighborhood. As his younger tag along, I guess you could say that he treated me like a typical American kid brother. Gene had a prosthetic leg that attached at the knee. A chance encounter one day after school with an unsupervised, reckless 8 year-old boy and a loaded 12-guage pump shotgun had cost him his leg. Now Gene had an amazing sense of humor when it came to his leg. He was the kind of kid who liked to use self-deprecating humor and keep everyone in stitches on the school bus. One of his favorite tricks was to pull the prosthetic limb behind his head as cars drove by, as if he was practicing some advanced form of yoga. He would pull until the leg came loose, and watch people nearly drive off the road in momentary disbelief. Another favorite gag of Gene's was to stick pens or pencils into his leg to get a rise out of anyone unfamiliar with him – anyone who didn't know that he was actually stabbing a prosthetic limb. After getting a laugh or two, without fail, Gene would turn to his intended audience and with a wink and a grin say "some people just know how to turn lemons into lemonade."

As a child, I realized early on that guns could be used for certain types of entertainment and family bonding rituals. At the same time, when used unwisely, they have the potential to lead to very bad things – or, in deference to Gene from the vignette above, a lot of lemons. Guns were something to always be respected and handled seriously and carefully, period. My family never had a great deal of involvement with guns, but we did have a tradition that included a family fowl hunting trip every September. Those are fond memories. My maternal Grandfather, Graham Martin, was also rumored to have been an incredible shot with a rifle. The story, as I've now heard it for over thirty years, and from at least a half a dozen sources, is that my Grandfather could shoot fowl, in flight, from a range of 150 feet or more, with a single-shot rifle. This is an impressive accomplishment, even with a shotgun at closer range. I also once watched as my uncle Terry did his best impersonation of Robert Redford in "Butch Cassidy and The Sundance Kid," by firing his double-action 22-caliber pistol nine times, rapidly, at a moving tuna fish can (at a distance of about 40 feet), hitting the can each time. What can I say? I was ten years old and I was impressed.

I freely admit that I stand somewhere close to the middle on guns and gun ownership. Both sides of the gun issue have problems. I have the firm belief that arming the ill-informed, reckless and grossly incompetent is a bad idea. As this research demonstrates, however, I am equally certain that contemporary gun control policy is based on very incomplete information about guns. What we do not know is what guns mean to the people who own and use them, beyond protection, an aspect of patriotism, freedom and the second amendment guarantee. We also do not fully understand how this translates directly into patterns of gun use. This is one of many questions to be explored within the pages of this book.

Guns have an undeniable significance and presence in the lives of Americans. The scientific community, and policy makers alike, however, repeatedly make one mistake where guns are concerned. The nature of this mistake or oversight is very simple. Take, for instance, any item that a person might have in their possession. Without exception, everything that we own takes on some meaning to us. Some items mean more than others, and these meanings are always based on our interaction with the items, the ways in which they have influenced or touched our lives, and their own sort of living histories. A person might own three baseball caps, mitts or bats, and regularly only use one of them. Why? The reasons are practically endless. Perhaps the owner pulled off some great athletic feat while using one in particular, and came to assign some special value to one over the others. Maybe the favored item was a gift from someone special. The point is this: as humans, we assign values to everything, and for a variety of reasons. In the end, however, the special values that we place on items and ideas influence the way that we behave, and the way that we interact with products, such as baseball caps, or anything else that we utilize. Guns are no exception to this rule. Every single gun has the potential to be valued differently, based on the gun's history, as well as the history of its owner and relative culture. Two identical guns, therefore, may come to be valued, interpreted and used differently, not only by two separate owners, but also by the same owner. As will be discussed at some length later, the use will be, in part, determined by the living history of the item in question.

Whereas there are a handful of scientific studies that have looked at the symbolic value of guns in the United States, they have proceeded with the incomplete premise that gun owners assign a universal meaning to all of their guns: protection, patriotism and freedom. This limited view overlooks a world of ritual activity and human emotion that determines how guns are defined and ultimately used. In order for social policy pertaining to the use of objects and ideas to be meaningful and effective, the symbolic values assigned to these objects, in motion, must first be understood, as these symbolic meanings will come to determine how objects – such as guns - are used in practice.

Relatively little has been published about the symbolic nature of guns and the ritualistic aspects of gun ownership in academic literature. While demographic facts of gun ownership have been extensively studied in the U.S. and abroad, the symbolic aspects of the guns and gun culture have been ignored. The purpose of this study is to explore aspects of U.S. gun culture about which little is known, in order to better understand this unique and inseparable part of our history as a common people. My research entails interviews conducted with U.S. gun owners about the history of the guns that make up their personal collections and the stories they tell about their guns. To emphasize, this project is about the cultural aspects of guns and gun collecting in the U.S. The guns evaluated in this book are considered cultural artifacts and discussed in terms of their symbolic value, historical significance, and cultural presentation. By learning more about how guns are thought about in the U.S. as symbols and as cultural artifacts, the researcher hopes to gain a better understanding of traditions, customs and other patterned behavior associated with guns and gun use. This, in turn, will usher in better-informed decisions regarding gun-related policies and procedures.

There is a sizeable body of literature suggesting that the cultural symbols that evolve out of every day social interaction serve to influence and regulate much of our behavior (Schaefer 2006; Seidman

2004; Geertz 1973; Durkheim 1965/1912). Although both material and non-material culture appear to be the products of social interaction, these social products (such as material goods, values and beliefs) are then assigned value and meaning that we use to communicate with one another and interact with our social and physical environments. In other words, although culture appears to be our creation, our creation is then used to regulate our behavior and actions in the form of complex rituals, customs and traditions that become integrated into our social institutions, social structure and socialization processes.

Consider Durkheim's (1965/1912) research on religion. He effectively demonstrated ways in which religious symbols and their meaning could be enhanced and perpetuated through seemingly mundane, even primitive local rituals. These primitive rituals and customs eventually diffused into mainstream, modern religious practices. For instance, whether U.S. citizens actively practice any form of organized religion, they cannot escape the far-reaching consequences of religion's symbolic influence. Religious symbolism is found in legal codes, social pleasantries, the architecture, and even the currency. So what does this have to do with guns? I am not arguing here that gun culture constitutes a religion. However, from a purely symbolic standpoint, religious artifacts help to illuminate the process by which individuals interact with cultural products, responding to and regulating behavior based on the perceived symbolic value of such artifacts (ex. a totem or crucifix).

Some modern ethnographical research efforts suggest that gender behavior, for instance, is heavily influenced by cultural symbols and their assigned gender values (Messner and Kimmel 2007; Connell 2005; Messerschmidt, 2000; West and Zimmerman 1987). Other recent research demonstrates how our understanding of culture and symbols directly influences our health, quality of life, and even life span (Courtenay 2000, Watson 2000; Messner 2000). Related research illustrates that guns are a masculine power symbol, or masculine gender currency that is used as props to perform certain forms of masculinity (Taylor 2009; Majors and Billison, 1992). More simply stated, our interaction with something as simple as a gun might influence the way gender is performed in a social context. As all forms of culture have symbolic meaning, all forms of culture communicate something to the social world. The symbolic meaning of any single piece of culture has the potential to influence the ways in which individuals interact with their social environments or audiences, using relevant and available aspects of culture as different type of performance-related props. There is nothing naturally masculine about motorcycles, for instance. They are just carbon structures, linked together by a series of metal and plastic components. Through their social presentations and various media portrayals, they have come to be seen as masculine objects, and a type of social prop that men can use to be "real men," or at least more manly – in certain contexts.

Therefore, on a general level, a more detailed understanding of gun culture might actually serve to explain the social mechanisms through which complicated social processes such as gender performances operate. Additionally, more specific to gun-related behavior, it has been suggested by Hoberman (2004) that even the simple representation of the symbolic meaning of guns and gun use, within the context of a movie (High Noon), has influenced the way in which several Presidential Administrations have conducted their affairs. If cultural artifacts like guns influence our behavior, and guns - due to their unique history, and constitutionally-guaranteed place within U.S. society – influence how we interact with one another and who we have come to be as a common people, then it is beneficial to know as much as possible about gun culture.

Whereas the symbolic value of guns has been largely ignored, extensive academic research has been dedicated to gun ownership. However, most of that literature deals with demographic characteristics associated with gun owners (Squires 2000), and seeks to determine who owns gun and for what purpose (Jiobu and Curry 2001; Stenross 1994; Lott 1998; Newton and Zimring 1969; Zimring and Hawkins 1987; and Zimring and Hawkins 1997). Similarly, the laws that regulate gun use are a matter of public record and well-documented. Notwithstanding, in light of recent landmark Federal Court rulings, such as the decision to overturn the 25-year Washington D.C. ban on handguns, public interests and debates pertaining to gun laws have been intensified and renewed in the areas of interpretation of gun laws, their histories, related appeals and implications (Korwin and Kopel 2008).

Although a few researchers have employed an ethnographic technique of sorts to study militias and the symbolic aspects of guns for defense (Poudrier 2001; Stenross 1994 and Squires 2000), there has been no notable focus on gun collectors and their stories. This is a group that deserves further attention from the academic community. When you want to know more about guns, logic seems to dictate that we must evaluate those who own and interact with them the most.

CHAPTER II

Gun Ownership is "Normal," Right?

Amy W. is an Associate Professor at a Midwestern liberal arts college who commented "I never considered myself "one of those gun people." After several years of a volatile and deteriorating relationship with her ex-husband, Amy suddenly became "very afraid…"

"He just went crazy. Doing and saying really bizarre things. He Would show up any time. Any place. I guess it was stalking. Out of the blue he wanted to get back together and wouldn't take no for an answer. I called the police and filed for a restraining order only after he became a little physical and threatened to harm himself, me and our son. After the restraining order he stopped coming to my home, but I would still see him out. He was always showing up somewhere down the street or around the corner, etc. After a while I think he was popping up in my sleep. I called the police to complain. They said they would talk to him again but he wasn't technically breaking the law again yet. I went to a local outdoors shop and bought a Smith & Wesson handgun. I was safe about it and took a few classes from a guy who taught lessons through the range at the store. I was surprised to find that discharging it… pulling the trigger was kind of exciting! Who knew? But the strangest part was when I told people I'd known for almost twenty years- close friends of mine – that I bought a gun, they looked at me like I was some sort of freak weirdo. You really could see the judgment in their faces. I was so sad. And I couldn't believe that I used to react the same way to other people who had guns. I just felt gross.

Tammy V. was a non-traditional college student. A single mom, Tammy started college in her late 50s. Life and circumstance had prevented her from beginning college out of high school. Instead, Tammy opted for life in the Military. She only served a few short years before becoming pregnant and being discharged of duty. Tammy enjoyed her time on the shooting range as a soldier, and purchased a handgun for household security and continued to shoot at local target ranges on occasion. She worked for her civilian employer, a local financial institution for fifteen years before revealing that she owned a gun.

"Well, it just never really came up. The office staff didn't talk guns much; but, when they did, it was usually in a negative light, depicting gun owners as the bad guy, and likely a bit crazy. One day one of the office workers said she and her husband had been robbed at knife point. I said too bad I wasn't there. I have a Glock 9mm. I'm pretty sure I could have taken a guy with a knife. You should have seen her face. She actually looked disgusted and wanted to know how I could own a gun. I reminded her that I had served in the military. That didn't bother her at all but the fact that I owned a gun did. It literally only took a few seconds for someone I had worked with for years to lump me into the same category as someone who had held her up at knife point. She had called the robber scummy, but it was written all over her face that I was scummy too. I just don't get that."

Amy and Tammy are, by no means, alone or abnormal in the least. A recent survey conducted by the United Nation's Office on Drugs and Crime reveals that the Unites States, which only accounts for about 5% of the world's population is believed to own and house approximately 50% of the working firearms on the planet. According the General Social Survey 1972-2006 cumulative data set, approximately 41.6% of U.S. households reported that guns were present. However, a 2011 report by the National Opinion Research Center (NORC) and Violence Policy Center (VPC) contend that the number of households in the United States reporting firearm ownership is steadily shrinking to closer to 32% of the population. While the report also showed a 10% decrease over the past 50 years in individual firearm ownership, what was clear is the extreme volume of guns still in circulation and high percentage of households reporting ownership.

Although the specific reasons for ownership are not entirely clear, these data indicate that a permissive attitude toward gun ownership is accepted by close to half of the U.S. adult population. This fact has received inadequate attention from the media, policy makers, the social sciences, and academic circles, in general. Even though gun ownership is so common and widespread, it has not generally been treated as a usual or "normal" occurrence by the scientific community. Instead, gun ownership and use has most typically been the subject of studies pertaining to crime and deviant behavior. What may come as a surprise to many, however, is that the overwhelming majority of known gun use is not deviant or criminal (Zimring and Hawkings 1997). This does not change the fact that scientific research efforts to understand gun behavior, such as use, ownership and presence, have relied almost exclusively on criminological theories and studies. This seems counterintuitive, applying theories developed to study criminal behavior to a legal practice undertaken by over a third of the adult U.S. population. In this book, I have shied away from the typical criminological focus on guns, and elected to focus more closely on the living histories, rituals, stigmatization, and the gender-related (masculinity) aspects of firearms that were revealed during the course of this project. I also seek to explore the issue of how and why men use guns as expressions or extensions of their masculinity, and ways in which this might provide a more detailed understanding of gun ownership and use, in addition to gender dynamics.

It is my contention that masculinity is primarily an achieved, socially constructed set of symbolic performances. As with any performance, depending on the delivery of the actor, and the circumstances and mood of the audience, success is often highly contextual (relative) and comes in varying degrees. The way we enact masculinity and femininity, succeeding and failing at our efforts, or what is sometimes called a "gender order," is not so different. Ubiquitous but quirky evidence of this reigning gender order in motion is colorfully depicted by Lee (2005), who delineates the protocol for what she terms a "man date." According to Lee's observations about the ways in which U.S. men interact in group contexts in which no woman is present, "a man date is two heterosexual men socializing without the crutch of business or sports. It is two guys meeting for the kind of outing a straight man might reasonably arrange with a woman. Dining together across a table without the aid of a television is a man date; eating at a bar is not. Taking a walk in the park together is a man date; going for a jog is not. Attending the movie "Friday Night Lights" is a man date, but going to see the Jets play is definitely not." Although Lee does not mention guns specifically, two men attending a gun show together or even participating in a shooting event together sometimes satisfies the requirements of a man date, as well, but ONLY if the men are there to talk about anything OTHER THAN guns – and especially if they are sharing their feelings and emotions about guns. As Connell (2000) indicates, however, there is no one global set of behaviors which conformed to, expressed or performed satisfy the requirements of some complete or total "masculinity.' Instead, there exists a variety of masculinities, arranged on a continuum of power, prestige, and status. What is yet to be fully explained, however, is how a "gender regime" or order, if primarily a social construct - and not some physical or biological reality - is established and so well-maintained among men, globally, and throughout history.

How does masculinity come to be portrayed (defined), acted out, and interpreted in everyday life? More specific to this work, where does gun ownership and use fit into the acceptance and practice of a gender order? Guns, whether viewed as fun play things, a means of protection, works of art, or instruments of death, also provide a rare, permissible playground of male emotional enactment and expression.

GUNS AND "THE COWBOY WAY"

Masculinity holds a special place in American life, and so do cowboys. Big screen icons which now resonate like ghosts from the past, such as John Wayne and Steve McQueen, are still alive and well in the American imagination. Social actors give special treatment to those who conform to conventional norms and express the same type of core masculine social values as the heroic, handsome and rugged cowboy, who never faltering, and unwaveringly honest, is always there to do the *right thing*, in the *right way*, and save the day. Even though there are varieties of masculinities – ranging from the dedicated, reliable dad to the gun-slinging cowboy - each separate form of hegemonic (prototypical/celebrated forms) masculinity holds a special, privileged place in American society, if not the world (and takes precedence to forms of femininity in the pecking order). As will be explored in some detail, these masculine privileges are gained at the expense of those who are considered less-than-masculine, and, in some instances, those unfortunate enough to enact these masculine forms rather than face public scrutiny, ridicule and social death.

Frances Olsen (1990) and Davidoff (1990) each suggested that our ancestors carved social life up into male and female spheres or domains when we were a more primitive (less specialized) species in order to protect women – primarily for population and general survival concerns. Olsen also argued that the long-term effect was that when formal social institutions later emerged amidst heightened specialization, the standardized framework of values that encapsulate each social institution reflected a gender-polarized world. Essentially, we had willingly and intentionally carved up the social world into male and female halves. The male half included forced emotional suppression, the arena of combat, hunting and the spoils of industry (ex, hands-on experience with all emergent technology). The female half, however, was relegated to the domestic arena, where an indulgence in emotions prevailed. Subsequently, males and females were socialized along slightly different paths. These separate paths included what would be cemented as a "gender hierarchy," and "sexualized dualisms" that overwhelmingly favored males and masculinities. In other words, as male and female social behavior patterns became increasingly more defined by their proximities to either the arenas of combat or the domestic arena, it was eventually taken for granted that these behavior differences were actually natural and not socially constructed differences. Over time, more positive connotations were associated with males, (and consequently masculinity) than females and femininity. For instance, males, actively engaged in the hunt, technology and combat, were more likely to be associated with courage, strength, honor, bravery, technical skills and logic. Conversely, females, protected in the domestic arena, were isolated from activities likely to lead to these gender associations, and often more likely to be viewed as frail, helpless, emotional, etc. The bottom line is that so many "cool" aspects of social life became the fun, gender playground for males, under the guise of "normal" masculinity, with little obvious comparable gender traits or expectations for females.,

Many aspects of masculinity, in general, are a highly valued part of social life. Performing "masculinities" through ritualistic, public and private acts is an important undertaking for men throughout the world. As will be addressed in chapter five, my data reveal that guns are often used to perform masculinity, and there are some unique rituals tied to masculinity that center around guns. So it is important to consider ways in which masculine privilege and prestige are awarded in some current day social contexts, especially when guns are involved.

It has been argued by theorists such as Michael Messner (2002), for instance, that sports offer one way for men to express their masculinity in a personal, individual way. Guns present a socially accepted way for men to accomplish this. Gun related activities, in general, are ripe with expression of masculinity. Firearms are also tools that have come to be used by some men as mechanisms or even masculine accessories by which to present and manage their emotions, exhibiting what I have come to think of throughout the course of this research as backyard or garage emotions.

Turner (2000) explains that we are emotion-driven beings. In turn, this world of emotions that makes up our daily lives has to be navigated and managed by all people. From birth, we are all taught the "appropriate" ways to manage our emotions. The rules for emotions vary by national, regional and local history, and even the specific social arena or context. Messner (2002) does a decent job of illustrating that males, in performing hegemonic forms of masculinity are socialized toward an acceptance of emotional suppression, accompanied by related "toxic consequences." These toxic consequences are played out in a variety of negative outcomes not experienced by women, free of the bonds of emotional suppression, to the same degree. Toxic consequences include heightened participation in violent behavior and accidents associated with participation in high-risk behaviors (Watson, 2000). As will be discussed and demonstrated through testimonials, collecting and shooting guns, however, also operates as one way for men to manage their suppressed emotions, and even, at times, allow their emotions to come out and play - in a "masculine" and appropriate manner, of course. Inversely, for women, it has been suggested by Browder (2006) that the persistent historical linking of both masculinity and citizenship to guns, is one way in which women have had difficulties in claiming or cashing in on the totality of their rights as a free citizen and patriot (234).

The activity and ritual surrounding gun ownership, collecting and shooting creates strong, passionate emotional bonds of a unique type. After all, many gun owners and enthusiasts regularly find themselves and their interests under fire, so to speak, in the popular media. The belief that you are protecting your heritage, freedom and a constitutional guarantee is, in and of itself enough to fuel a strong connection among like-minded individuals, those who feel embattled. Interestingly, the nature of shooting sports, although permissive of a certain brand of emotional exchanges, also demands that the highly charged emotions that many feel in relation to their guns and their use are controlled and kept in check. Naturally, this cool control is necessary for the sake of safety and accuracy. What is clearly evidenced in this systematic display of forced, emotional suppression, is a sort of template for traditional, celebrated masculinity. There is also an unspoken dismissal of a feminine approach to handling guns, which would typically promote the sharing of feelings and emotions. As a part of this prototypical, normal cowboy masculine world, it is clear that men like their guns. They like collecting, holding, shooting, cleaning, and as I've discovered, sometimes even smelling them – all of which have led to the development of some unique social rituals of a masculine type that center around guns. These rituals will be the specific focus of the latter chapters.

THE GENDER PERFORMANCE

Whether gender is socially constructed, an extension of genetic coding, or a little bit of each, is a crucial and unsolved scientific mystery. In this book, I support the contemporary view that masculinities are something individuals have to constantly work to achieve, based on available resources or props (social symbols) that have come to be associated with some aspect of being the right kind of man. According to Connell (2000), gender differentiation, the process wherein the assumed biological differences between males and females are assigned specific social value, is influenced by often antiquated gender ideologies. These out-of-date ideologies are instrumental in influencing the expectations surrounding male and female emotions and related behavior. Contemporary masculinity is popularly viewed now as an actively achieved status among men, incorporating the suggestion by West and Zimmerman (1987:126) that:

> When we view gender as an accomplishment, an achieved property of situated behavior, our attention shifts from matters internal to the individual and focuses on interactional and, ultimately, institutional arenas.

Similarly, the processes of "legitimation" and "reification," as described by Peter Berger and Thomas Luckmann (1966) help to illuminate this type of phenomena. They contend that much of what we accept as "objective" reality or fact is actually a "fragile reality," or reified concept that has come to appear as naturally occurring - due to the combined abilities and collaborative efforts of various agents of social institutions in making them appear legitimate. More specifically, they argue that the effective use of history, philosophy, science, etc., makes us less likely to see the man behind the curtain. The final products are aspects of social life and forms of social control that are not intrinsically real; however, they have very real consequences in terms of our lives and life outcomes.

Within the framework of this study, I seek an understanding of how the past experiences of boys and men impact their current and future behavior – with special consideration to gun-related behavior. More specifically, I consider how past social constructions of masculine symbols, values and beliefs are packaged, altered, marketed, refined, and used in motion, as part of everyday, lived lives, to reconstruct a new masculine identity in present or possibly future forms. All constructions and reconstructions of masculinity explored in this study are framed within the context of contemporary U.S. gun culture.

MANAGING AND NEGOTIATING EMOTIONS

Guns are indeed a highly emotional topic, on many levels. The ways in which guns facilitate the harnessing, controlling, channeling and sometimes re-directing of emotions allows for an intricate web of male activities. Although many gun owners and collectors will describe the value of a gun based on special properties (such as serial number, unique design or limited availability) that give it a fixed and specific market or monetary value, borrowing from Durkheim (1965/1912), I am more interested in exploring the symbolic, emotional value that gun owners and collectors place on their guns. According to Durkheim (1965/1912), a vested *emotional*, symbolic value of an object or idea is a unique product of social interaction that centers around the concepts of respect and majesty. "To be sure, in the sentiment which the believer feels for the things he adores, there is always fear derived from respect and the dominating emotion of majesty" (79). Emotions indicative of this "awe inspiring majesty" and pride will be covered in some detail.

How do the emotions that center on gun activities translate directly into behavior? Although the base of knowledge in this area is far more theoretical than applied, the dominant view of emotions is that they influence the way men see and interpret the world and organize patterns of thought. According to Turner (2000), emotions are highly complex, organized, meaningful systems of adaptation. It is important to note here, before continuing, that I do not necessarily accept Turner's model of emotion in its entirety. He does not offer clear evidence demonstrating that at some point in our biological evolution that genetic or "hard wired" emotion later gave way to socially constructed influences (77). It seems equally likely to me, that the way in which humans or any organism interacts with their social and physical environments could, in turn influence the physical properties of the organism and its subsequent offspring. What I admire about Turner's explanation of the development and dynamics of human emotion, is that it really does not matter which came first, the end results may well be the same: Emotion matters! As humans evolve both socially and biologically and emotional expression becomes more complex and diversified, the species is improved - social institutions and related social structures become more stable, and our odds of long-term survival increase (43 and 49). "The more varied are the forms of sociality and solidarity that can be created and sustained; and the more flexible are the social relations formed, the more fitness-enhancing are these relations" (43). In the end, it is neither the biological or social origin of emotion that matters, but the undeniable presence and significance of emotion in day to day interaction. As Turner colorfully illustrates

> Even after millions of years of evolution expanding the capacity of hominids to mobilize more varied emotional states, social interaction among humans still requires the use of emotion-arousing rituals.....Why so? Virtually all theories of interpersonal processes among humans recognize that interactions start with ritual openings and closings, with additional rituals for tracking the flow of emotional energy...for repairing breaches, sustaining or shifting topics and other features of interaction...Thus, the mobilization and release of emotional energy in humans still needs a source of ignition for jump-starting an interacting...Even after millions of years of evolution...humans are still not able to

spontaneously mobilize their interpersonal energies without rituals (Turner, 2000:44).

Tying this directly to gun ownership and use, the argument being presented is that emotions directly influence the way that men use or interact with their guns. At this point, there is no reason to suppose that this would not also hold true for gun-related behavior and actions on both the group and individual level. As Arlie Hochschild described in her famous (1983) essays on emotion management, the so-called "feeling rules," which are publically acted out and socially sanctioned are channeled into narrow, "gender specific" emotions. In terms of the specific relevance to guns, their use provides men one rare outlet to redirect and channel their often suppressed emotions. The acts of shooting, and, as will be discussed, gun celebrating, are conducted using the available and approved symbolic representations of masculinity in U.S. society and culture discussed in the preceding sections.

These emotional outlets, or the way that guns are used, displayed, presented, and talked about will be found where men live, work and play together. For instance, in Tim O'Brien's (1999) "The Things They Carried," he describes a man reluctant to go to war even when drafted. For an American man, refusing to take up arms is considered by many to be an act of extreme cowardice and lack of both character and patriotism. It's just not the John Wayne way; it is not being "the right kind of cowboy." It is difficult in contemporary U.S. society to identify a comparable dilemma for females, in general.

WARRIOR NARRATIVES

Contemporary studies in the area of gender have revealed that, on a general level, the indoctrination into gun use intersects gender socialization and the learning of masculinities. This process is underscored by recent explorations of "warrior narratives." Socialization, which encapsulates a lifelong learning process, entails how standardized attitudes, values and beliefs are culturally transmitted and influence behavioral patterns. Of central importance in socialization is the perpetuating of the symbolic meaning/value of various aspects of both material and non-material culture for incorporation into social performances. Warrior narratives are the running scripts lived out by individual social actors that unfold during the course of performing some aspect of masculinity (Jordan and Cowan 2007). Jordan and Cowan (2007) focused on the warrior narratives used by children in a Kindergarten classroom to negotiate aspects of gender along a variety of basic tasks, leisure activities and general social exchanges. They found that the performance of masculinity was facilitated by learned, symbolic aspects of masculinity as expressed through the codes of warrior narratives, and used to play even basic childhood games. For instance, a male child playing with a toy car was likely to engage in a running narrative about how it was involved in a police chase or some deviant act – where no such warrior narratives were found to be expressed while engaging in activities not typically associated with traditional forms of masculinity (ex. girls playing with dolls). Further evidence of masculinity narratives have been explored by Evans and Wallace (2008), who found that male prisoners, upon reflection of their own upbringings, and what it "means to be a man" found the persistent presence of varied warrior narratives in each of the prisoners' accounts. These narratives included similar themes of "emotional suppression," "hardness," "power," and the necessary audience perception of strength (no weakness) at all times. Similarly, Hutchings (2008), in her analysis of masculinity and war has noted that the active role of war narratives, and the related incorporation into masculine performance are inseparably linked (i.e. as definitions of one changes, the other is adapted to be complementary).

These narratives are very similar to what Mills and Tivers (2001) and Hunt (2008) describe as living histories. Typically referring to past events that are reconstructed through "serious leisure," with a specific place (such as a battlefield) in mind, a living history

> constitutes a collective attempt to recreate historical events on designated sites through replicating…a particular period by actors living out the conditions of the day (Mills and Tivers 2001:1; Hunt 2008: 461).

Hunt argues that "traditional masculinities" are "negotiated and manufactured" through a "site of a serious leisure pursuit that attempts to draw boundaries with the feminine" (Hunt 2008: 460). Here she is talking about specific sites, such as battlefields, where a known type of masculinity is actively performed, through the leisure of detailed outdoor performance – with an effort to do the masculinity in an historically accurate way. Warrior narratives, interestingly, achieve essentially the same basic ends, with actual research subjects, in real time, providing living narratives surrounding any specific place, activity or aspect of culture (such as a gun) that the researcher is lucky enough to observe. In the case of the gun, it becomes a type of historical site, and narratives surrounding its use may be captured and analyzed to provide insight into socialization pertaining to guns, and gun culture, in general.

GUN LAWS "IN THE NEWS"

As this book is unfolding, guns are everywhere in the public psyche and lexicon – guns are a hot topic. On July 20, 2012, during the midnight movie premier of *The Dark Knight Rises* in a crowded Aurora, CO, theatre, James Holmes allegedly opened fire, killing 12 and injuring 58 more. He was also said to have been dressed in a suit of body armor and referring to himself as the cartoon movie villain, the Joker. The trial and investigations are still under way, and no specific motivation for the killings and method of killing is known as of this printing.

This tragedy comes on the heels of other highly-publicized shootings in recent years. After being denied tenure, Biology Professor Amy Bishop walked into a Department meeting at the University of Alabama at Huntsville in February, 2010. She was armed with a 9mm pistol, and opened fire, killing three Professors and wounding three others. Bishop pleaded guilty to the charge of murder to avoid capital punishment and was sentenced to life. She could also still face a trial in her home state of Massachusetts, where she has been belatedly charged in the 1986 killing of her 18-year-old brother. Originally Seth Bishop's death had been ruled an accident, as his sister Amy Bishop indicated that the shotgun, which belonged to their father had accidentally discharged repeatedly in the family home as she tried to unload it. In light of the Alabama shootings, the investigation of the Massachusetts shooting was re-opened by prosecutors, pending the outcome of the case in Alabama.

On February 14, 2008, a former graduate student walked into a classroom at Northern Illinois University, opened fire and killed six. December 2007, a gunman opened fire in a Colorado Springs church, killing two. Two more were killed on the same day, 70 miles away in Arvada, Colorado, when a gunman opened fire in a youth ministry dormitory. These shootings occurred on the heels of two other highly publicized shootings. The first was the Virginia Tech Massacre on April 16, 2007, resulting in 32 deaths. Also, on February 8, 2008, a woman opened fire in a classroom at the Louisiana Technical College, killing three. In October of 2007, an Ohio teen shot both of his parents in the head, resulting in the death of his mother, in response to his video game privileges being revoked. An 8eight- year-old boy ambushed and killed his father and his father's friend in November, 2008, in St. John's Arizona. In January 2008, a four-year-old boy in Jackson, Ohio pulled a loaded 12-guage shotgun out of a closet and shot his 18-year-old babysitter in retaliation for the babysitter accidentally stepping on the child's foot. Generating more of a buzz than these highly publicized shootings, however, is new legislation and Supreme Court activity pertaining to the interpretation of the 2nd Amendment and related gun laws.

While this list, unfortunately, is just a sample, and far-from exhaustive, such incidents are not limited to the United States. On July 22, 2011, mass murderer Anders Behring Breivik claimed 77 victims in Norway. Dressed in a fake police uniform, Breivik hunted down and assassinated children at the Labour Party youth camp on Utoeya island. Breivik insisted that he was sane, and declared his crimes to all have been legitimate acts of political protest and was ultimately convicted of terrorism and premeditated murder. He was given the maximum sentence of twenty-one years imprisonment.

With all of the carnage mentioned at the beginning of this section - which doesn't come close to accounting for a fraction all of the gun-related violence during the same time period - it would be natural to anticipate a tightening of restrictions pertaining to gun ownership and use. In fact, the polar opposite appears to be the case. According to MSNBC, on April 9, 2008, Florida Law Makers approved new legislation permitting workers who own guns to take them to work and keep them in their automobiles – even if the owners of the private property do not permit the guns. Some types of workplaces, such as nuclear power plants, prisons, schools and companies whose business involves homeland security were exempted, however, due to obvious safety concerns. More center-stage in a non-stop barrage of 24-hour news cycles is the decision made by the U.S. Supreme Court, to revisit a landmark case from 1976, which banned handgun ownership in Washington D.C. in reaction to what was then perceived to be an epidemic of interpersonal violence. According to a September 24, 2007, report issued by the Cato Institute:

on September 4, the District of Columbia government asked the Supreme Court to reverse a federal appellate decision in *Parker v. District of Columbia*, 478 F.3d 370 (D.C. Cir. 2007), which upheld a Second Amendment challenge to D.C.'s ban on all functional firearms. The six D.C. residents who brought the lawsuit — although they won in the lower court — agree with the city that the Supreme Court should revisit the Second Amendment *for the first time since 1939.* A four-square pronouncement from the High Court is long overdue. The entire nation, not just Washington, D.C., needs to know how courts will interpret "the right of the people to keep and bear arms." Sometime before year end, the justices will decide whether to review the case. If the Supreme Court chooses to intervene, a final decision will probably be issued by June 30, 2008.

At the heart of the interpretation issue is the meaning of the 27 famous - if not troublesome - words from the 2nd Amendment of the Constitution of the United States of America: ""A well regulated militia, being necessary to the security of a free State, the right of the people to keep and bear Arms shall not be infringed." On June 26, 2008, The U.S. Supreme court, for the first time, interpreted the "core ambiguity" of the Second Amendment's wording, in deciding the District of Columbia v Heller case, with a 5-4 ruling that opted in favor of the constitutionally protected right of individuals to own handguns (www.msnbc.msn.com/id/25390404). The overall impact of this reversal of a thirty-year ban on handguns in Washington D.C. and other major U.S. cities is yet to be determined. However, for the moment, a nation that already stakes a claim to well over 200,000,000 guns has further strengthened its position on the right to own them.

Emma Schwartz (2008), along with the Brady Campaign to Prevent Gun Violence (http://www.bradycampaign.org), indicates that most Americans would be surprised to find out how few pieces of comprehensive Federal gun legislation have actually been handed down since the signing of the constitution. Quite literally, there has only been a handful to date. It is important to note, however, that it has taken tremendous social chaos, social panic, and a few major socio-political events to spark sufficient interest and support to pass existing gun laws.

To further illustrate the escalating public attention and concern pertaining to guns and gun use in the last century, Alan Korwin (1995) mapped out the "growth" in Federal gun laws from 1791 to 1994. As illustrated in table 2.1 and chart 2.1, although the figures are crude, based only on the amount of words added to United States Federal Laws (new and existing), he effectively demonstrates a lack of attention to or interest in major changes to gun legislation from 1791 until public fear driven largely by heightened public concern and awareness of organized crime violence prompted the passage of the National Firearms Act of 1934 and Federal Firearms Act of 1938. For the first time, the National Firearms Act imposes a tax on the sale and transfer of machine guns and short-barrel firearms, including sawed-off shotguns. Passed immediately following the end of Prohibition, the law was not well received by notorious gangsters of the time, like John Dillinger and Al Capone (Schwartz 2008). The Federal Firearms Act of 1938 was not as broad in scope as the National Firearms Act, but it was the first piece of legislation requiring gun dealers to obtain a Federal license. As depicted in chart 2.1, we then see little change until public reaction over highly publicized acts of violence, such as the assassinations of John F. Kennedy, Robert Kennedy and Martin Luther King usher in the 1968 Gun Control Act. This was followed by a series of acts in response to increased fear of violent crime surrounding the unparalleled, escalating Federal spending phenomenon that would come to be known as the war on drugs.

The candidates of U.S. presidential elections in the mid-1960's focused on the restoration of peace, law and order to the streets of rural and urban America. These clean-up efforts were a response to strong public outcries against escalating crime rates. The resulting 1968 Gun Control Act adds a variety of restrictions on gun sales, purchasing and ownership. This body of legislation achieves expanded licensing and record-keeping requirements (such as requiring serial numbers on all firearm, requiring licensed dealers to keep records of firearm transactions and authorizing federal officials to inspect dealers records and inventory), bans some assault weapons and "Saturday Night Specials," while prohibiting those with felony crime records, drug addicts, minors, anyone dishonorably discharged from military service, illegal immigrants, those who have forfeited their U.S. citizenship and the mentally ill from buying guns. The sale of mail-order firearms was also banned, including rifles and shotguns for the first time (Schwartz 2008).

Chart 2.1: Federal Changes to U.S. Gun Laws from 1791to 1994

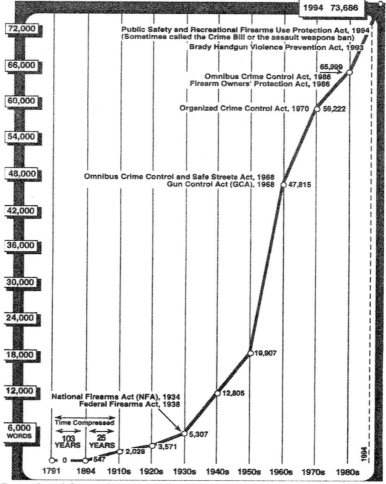

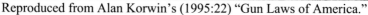

Reproduced from Alan Korwin's (1995:22) "Gun Laws of America."

Table 2.1: Tracking New Federal Gun Law Legislation from 1791 to 1994

Growth in Federal Gun Laws: The Numbers

DATE	Words added	New USC sections	% increase at the time	% of total as of 1994
1791	0*	0	—	0
1894	547	1	—	0.7
1910s	1,481	7	271	2.0
1920s	1,543	8	43.2	2.1
1930s	1,736	9	32.7	2.4
1940s	7,498	37	58.6	10.2
1950s	7,102	42	35.7	9.6
1960s	27,908	51	58.4	37.9
1970s	11,407	26	19.3	15.5
1980s	6,777	28	10.3	9.2
1994	7,687	22	10.4	10.4
Totals	73,686	231		

*The 27 words of the Second Amendment (and other Constitutional provisions) are not statutes and are not counted for the purposes of this chart.

Reproduced from Alan Korwin's (1995:22) "Gun Laws of America."

This opened the door for Federal intervention into state law enforcement in the U.S. The establishment of the Law Enforcement Assistance Administration (LEAA) signaled a new, strong presence of the federal government in local law enforcement efforts and the LEAA established an Office of Law Enforcement in the Department of Justice. The Bureau of Alcohol, Tobacco, and Firearms (ATF) was created in 1972. The function of this bureau is monitoring and regulating the sale of guns. By the early 1980s, serious reform was underway, including some rethinking of prior Federal legislation. In 1986, the McClure-Volkmer Act (Also Known As the Firearms Owners Protection Act) repealed several requirements of the 1968 Gun Control Act discussed above. Some of the deep cutting reforms included a reversal in position on: ammunition sale by mail; ammunition record keeping; and protection from arrest for travelers with properly stored firearms. McClure-Volkmer did, however, include a ban of the sale of machine guns made after May 19, 1986 to private persons. Then, in 1993, the Brady Handgun Prevention Act was passed, requiring gun dealers to run background checks on purchasers and gun purchases. The act also leads to the creation of a national database of firearm purchases. One major limitation to the Brady legislation, however, is that it creates a "loophole" where private or individual owners/sellers are not required to run similar checks or maintain database records for sales and transfers.

Although it would be allowed to lapse 10 years later, in 1994, the Violent Crime Control and Law Enforcement Ban was passed, which banned the sale of new assault weapons. Some innovative legislation, the Tiahrt Amendment, was introduced in 2003, ensuring the anonymity of gun purchasers and prohibiting the disclosure of" trace data" about guns used in crimes, and offers extended protection to gun dealers who are not directly involved in crimes that may result from guns that they sell. Additionally, in 2007, pursuant to the wave of crimes mentioned at the beginning of this section, a technological advancement in gun legislation allowed for improvements to the "National Instant Criminal Background System (ICBS)."

The general idea is that as database records of those known to be prohibited from purchasing firearms (ex. Such as felons and the mentally ill), will be integrated into the ICBS and shared with licensed merchants and law enforcement agencies.

In terms of changes and costs involved, a (1994) special issue of Congressional Digest mapped out the evolution of the Federal Law Enforcement roles and related crime budgets (in part driven by public fear of gun violence), noting that "since 1965, the expenditure of Federal funds rose from $535 million to $11.7 billion in fiscal Year 1992, an increase of over 2,000%" (1994:162). At the same time, on the local level, Washington, D.C. and New York City each passed the strict and now famous gun control statutes that outlawed the possession of handguns, in most cases, within those cities. Again, this was fear-driven legislation; however, in these instances, the fear was of the guns themselves, and the violence they enabled. . As chart 2.2 illustrates, although gun-related violent crimes have significantly declined over the past 20 year, and only account for about 10% of known violent crime since 1993, this still means over 300,000 citizens report facing an attacker with a firearm each year (see Chart 2.3). This does not change the fact, however, that contrary to heightened media-driven concern over highly-publicized public shootings, overall, gun violence is down. In 1997, researchers Zimring and Hawkins expand on the link between fear and gun activity, arguing that it is not simply the presence of guns that leads to increased violence, but the presence of guns in the wrong type of social climate or context. While gaining a precise understanding of specifically which contexts and social conditions breed all forms of violence remains problematic, there does appear to bit of a changing tide in relation to percentage of U.S. households owning guns, as well as a downward trend in violence overall (see Chart 2.4).

Chart 2.2: Gun Crime Decline for past 20 years

Gun Crime Declines for Past 20 Years	1993	2010	Source
Gun Homicides Per 100,000 People	7.0	3.6	CDC
Gun Homicide Deaths	18,253	11,078	CDC
Non-Fatal Gun Crime Vicitimization	1.5 Million	467,000	NCVS
Non-Fatal Gun Crime Vicitimization Per 100,000 People	725.3	181.5	NCVS
Property Crimes Per 100,000 People	351.8	138.7	NCVS

*The violent crimes included are rape and sexual assault, robbery, and aggravated assault
Source: Bureau of Justice Statistics, National Crime Victimization Survey (NCVS) 1993-2011. Ongoing since 1972 with a redesign in 1993, this survey of households interviews about 134,000 persons age 12 and older in 77,200 households twice each year about their victimizations from crime. The source for Gun Homicides Per 100,000 people and Gun Homicide Death estimates: Center For Disease Control and Prevention.

Many prominent studies have demonstrated that older, white, middle class men are the primary owners of guns (Kleck 1991), but they have failed to evaluate the reasons and symbolic meaning behind guns, gun ownership, and gun use in a notable way. To be sure, the survey data upon which most of this research is anchored is useful for compiling more accurate figures on household gun ownership. The major problem, however, and what is still a great mystery, is one of causality. Most gun-related studies have extrapolated conclusions about guns and gun owner' characteristics by using General Social Survey (GSS) Data, from a large, multi-stage probability sample of households in the United States. The value of these data, are that much like census data, GSS questionnaires touch on a wide range of useful topics. The questionnaire, which has been administered since 1972, generally bi-yearly, is administered using cross sectional samples. The downside, however, is that GSS data are not particularly well-suited for or designed specifically to study gun owners.

Chart 2.3: Nonfatal firearm victimization, 1993-2011

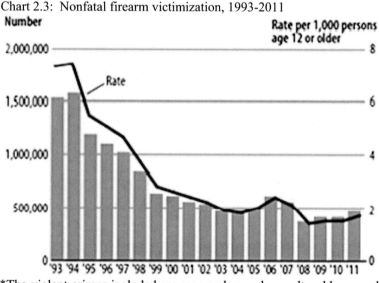

*The violent crimes included are rape and sexual assault, robbery, and aggravated assault

Source: Bureau of Justice Statistics, National Crime Victimization Survey (NCVS) 1993-2011.

Chart 2.4: Violence in America, 1960-2010

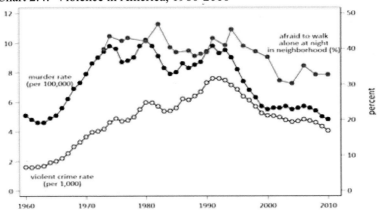

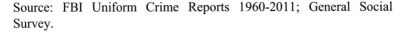

Source: FBI Uniform Crime Reports 1960-2011; General Social Survey.

At present, pinpointing the causal sequence or gun ownership and/or related violence is impossible to accomplish using available research methods and statistical models. At best, studies must be driven by intuition and creativity. What is arguably the most innovative attempt to disentangle the causal sequence of fear driving gun ownership was undertaken by Curry and Jiobu (2001), who found that even when controlling for a whole host of other factors that influence gun ownership (ex Income, education, region, religion, city size, political ideologies, etc.) a side effect of fear remains in the form of a lack of confidence. Those who lack confidence or fear the government or its inability to protect them are more likely to own guns.

CONCEAL AND CARRY

One area where both fear and lack of confidence in the Federal Government have shown up readily in the patterns of the general population and related paradigm shift at the state level is the concealed carry laws – or in some jurisdictions and states, Carrying a Concealed Weapon (CCW). Currently the right to obtain concealed carry permits is not addressed directly by Federal law. However, Illinois is currently the only U.S. state that does not have some state-level mechanism in place to grant at least provisional conceal and carry permits to individual civilians. The other 49 states have passed a variety of laws allowing citizens to carry specified concealed firearms in public, under certain conditions. There is considerable variation among states, but permit requirements generally include proof of U.S. and issuing state residency, age restrictions, background check/fingerprinting, completion of a certified handgun/firearm safety class, demonstrating handgun proficiency, and processing and/or licensing fees. These requirements vary widely by jurisdiction, with some having only some or none of these requirements and others having most or all of them. While Federal Law does not explicitly grant or disallow the right to obtain conceal and carry permits, one typical example of the restrictive conditions at the state level directly pertains to the guiding hand of Federal Law. The Gun-Free School Zones Act (GFSZA), enacted as section 1702 of the Crime Control Act of 1990, strictly limits where an unlicensed person may carry a firearm (openly or concealed). Within 1000 feet of a school zone is prohibited, but exceptions are granted to holders of valid State-issued weapons permits. Most states require a permit, while a handful, such as Alaska, Vermont and Arizona do not.

Prior to 1995, the majority of U.S. states were either designated as "No Issues," meaning that with very few exceptions, conceal and carry permits were not issued to civilians, or they were "May Issue" designated, indicating that permits were issued on a limited, case-by-case basis. The standards for issuance were inconsistent, with policies that were highly subjective and varied widely from state-to-state, and even from one county to the next. Since the mid-1990s, most states have moved toward more standardized licensing practices, but also towards a less-restrictive "Shall Issue" designation. "Shall-Issue" jurisdictions require conceal and carry permits to carry a handgun, but, the process is more streamlined, and the criteria for determination are specified in the individual state laws. Unlike the local or regional discretion allowed under "May Issue" guidelines, none is granted in "Shall Issue" states; and, there is also no requirement of the applicant to demonstrate "good cause" or need to conceal and carry a gun. In sum, the laws in "Shall-Issue" jurisdictions generally indicate that an issuing body or authority *shall issue* permits if all state-mandated criteria are met. Alternately, *may issue permits are,* at least partially, at the discretion of the local issuing authority.

State "reciprocity" is another key consideration in conceal and carry laws. There is so much variation among and within different states, it can be very difficult for a licensed civilian to know if they are in compliance with State law if they are planning to travel with their guns and cross state lines (or planning to get licensed in or by a state where they do not reside). In practice, reciprocity among states is very similar to extradition agreements between states and nations. One state will enter into an agreement with others wherein, all participating parties agree to honor permits or licenses issued by other jurisdictions with similar standards on a restricted and limited basis. The precise recognition of concealed carry privileges and rights varies widely from one state to another. The majority of U.S. states currently have reciprocity agreements with at least one state, and some honor permits issued by all states.   One new innovation in conceal and carry reciprocity was passed by Utah in 2011. For non-Utah residents who now apply for an out-of-state license, they must first provide proof that they have a current conceal and carry permit in their own state of residence. For a more complete picture of the current conceal and carry designation and reciprocities, see Appendix A.

A FRESH APPROACH

Fear and paranoia may be a primary motivator for gun owners seeking conceal and carry permits. This gives us little insight as to how these guns sometimes come to be used in problematic ways. A new approach to studying gun ownership suggested in this project will aid policy makers in their understanding and treatment of volatile issues surrounding gun use and ownership. A better understanding of the real experiences and belief of gun owners and supporters will bring us closer to realistic expectations concerning gun control and practical solutions.   I also suggest that previous research efforts exercise an incomplete and faulty logic by focusing too narrowly on the connection between gun volume, personal injury and violence in general.   The assumption that more guns equal more violence proceeds with the premise that each gun is equally likely to be used to commit an act of violence. I argue that the living history and symbolic value ascribed to each gun has a direct influence on the outcomes associated with each gun. As emphasized by Zimring and Hawkins (1997), one size fits all policies won't work. Different regions, states, counties, cities, neighborhoods and even households have different concerns – each potentially influenced separately by the presence and active use of guns). Additionally, as some of my project data will reveal, many gun owners who own a large number of guns not only are not criminal, they express an overtly hostile and proactively reactionary stance that they would never deign to use a gun in any threatening, unsafe or disrespectful manner.

I further propose that the interactive world of the gun presents a seamless tango, simultaneously characteristic of fear, disdain, pride and love. As my data reveal in the later chapters, a gun owner might claim that guns, in general, mean "a right to bear arms," or indicate which specific guns within their collection represent added security to protect their families or serve as reminders of special memories of loved ones - while others are used as ceremonial rites of passage, and pathways of emotional exchanges among males. The world of the gun is a busy and expressive world, and far more involved than existing literature or social policy would suggest. This gap between policy and reality must be acknowledged, understood and reconciled through scientific study.

CHAPTER III

Making Science Out of Gun Ownership

As Ferrell And Hamm (1998) adroitly observed, at times, an effort to be too scientific in our approach to studying social behavior puts us at risk of diminishing our efforts; robbing us of the richness and potential of some of the more heated and complex subject matter. I endeavored to heed their warning, being ever mindful of providing as much detail as possible throughout this study. Although IRB (Institutional Review Board) considerations made studying illegal aspects of gun ownership impractical, the social sensitivity and consternation surrounding my subject matter presented a series of compromising situations and special challenges. Most of these challenges are addressed in the chapter on stigma, and include issues such as mistrust and overt hostility. As the behavior under review is not illegal, complicit behavior was not a necessary component of the research; however, at times, performing or going along with the activities being studied enabled the researcher to gain access and perspective.

Whether the participant feels that the stigma associated with their pastimes pigeonhole them as a "wacko revolutionary" or someone that poses an immediate threat that "must be disarmed," a language of mistrust has become an inseparable part of the gun collecting and live action cowboy club identity. To illustrate, one informant, having just met the investigator, began a pre-interview conversation by asserting "you probably think that we are nuts for owning guns, right?" This was typical of conversations with new subjects who participate in these groups, indicative of the notion that everyone on the outside, or part of mainstream values believes that these participants are flawed and dangerous. As a result, gun culture participants have become guarded, and trust must be established before admission is granted. They have to know where those unfamiliar to these circles stand on certain gun issues, and sometimes how individuals react in the physical presence of guns. Participating in the "serious" leisure of gun collecting and live-action tournaments requires more than a simple willingness and commitment on the part of the participant: it also requires the *admission, authentication* and *acceptance* of gate-keepers within the subculture. This process is illuminated through the helpful observations of a female live action cowboy target shooter at an event in Chillicothe, Ohio. The researcher was having difficulty establishing communication with participants (or having no luck finding anyone willing to be interviewed). Upon recognizing the researcher's predicament, she offered up the following:

> You know, if you actually hold a gun, more of them will talk
> to you (admission). If you shoot, some of them will start to
> trust you (authentication), and if you actually hit something,
> they're all yours (acceptance).

Ferrell and Hamm's approach to "criminological verstehen" was also useful in attempting to locate the subjective aspects of guns; situational meanings, emotions portrayed by the actors involved, and broader social contexts in which the gun-related activities under study take place.

The findings reported in this book have emerged in the context of a multi-method fieldstudy, also employing Clifford Geertz' "thick, descriptive" style of observing and characterizing data in motion, with grounded theoretical techniques. The late Clifford Geertz challenged us in his seminal (1973) work "The Interpretation of Cultures," to recognize that it is essential for a qualitative researcher to go beyond making "thin" descriptions of our observed data, and sharpen our focus to ferret out a rich, "thick description" of whatever is unfolding around us. Geertz explains that an observer witnessing a research subject closing only one eye might produce a "thin description" by documenting it as merely a twitch. Upon closer scrutiny, however, a more astute, culturally imbedded or well-informed researcher might have seen the same "thin" twitch as a piece of coded information, communicating a variety of possible meanings (such as a wink meaning anything from "I know something you don't know," the acknowledgement that secret information has been exchanged, a form of flirtation, etc.) to his or social audience (Geertz 1971:6-9; Ryle 1971). Geertz encouraged us to position ourselves as researchers in such a way as to best facilitate wading through the "winks upon winks," and arrive at informed, thick descriptions that unveil often veiled codes and categories of shared meaning. Toward this end, I have found tenets of grounded theory to be the best suited to this cultural study of gun owners.

The purpose of grounded theory is to discover social theory by systematically collecting and analyzing data, and locating themes, categories and relationships among the data, social contexts and concepts (Glaser 1992; Charmaz 2006). It is left to the skill, training, preparedness and creative flexibility of the researcher to identify a research question, study relevant data, and ultimately identity theoretical categories that emerge after careful reflection and consideration of the data. Once arrived at, the grounded theoretical product will be presented as either a set of well-documented and detailed set of "codified propositions," or in an ongoing, fluid, "theoretical discussion" unfolding from the data, relying on emergent "conceptual categories and their properties" (Glasser and Strauss 1967: 31).

For the purpose of generating grounded theory, the researcher plays a crucial role. A finely tuned, observant and motivated researcher is essential to this process. As stated by Glasser and Strauss (1967:251):

> The researcher is a highly sensitized and systematic agent. The researcher has insights, and he can make the most of them...through systematic comparative analysis.

In order to facilitate the process of moving from a trained researcher's observations of data to related, emergent theory, Glaser and Strauss (1967) envisioned grounded theory as emphasizing two primary procedures: a constant comparative method, and theoretical sampling (Charmaz 2006). Charmaz (2006) explains the constant comparative method to be

> A method of analysis that generates successively more abstract concepts and theories through inductive processes of comparing data with other data... emerging categories with other emerging categories and categories with concepts. These

Comparisons are then used to signal each stage of analytic development. (187).

This method helps to keep the researcher engaged in the project, and enhance the prospects of yielding more fruitful outcomes. According to Glaser and Strauss (1967) theoretical sampling essentially entails the fluid processes of observing/collecting, coding and analyzing the data. Charmaz (2006) elaborates on theoretical sampling for the purpose of constructing grounded theory a little more, by asserting that

> ...the researcher aims to develop the properties of his or her developing categories and themes, not to sample randomly selected populations or to sample representative distributions of a particular population. When engaging in theoretical sampling, the researcher seeks people, events, or information to illuminate and define the boundaries and relevance of the categories. Because the purpose of theoretical sampling is to sample and discover the theoretical categories, conducting it can take the researcher across multiple substantive areas (189).

Theoretical sampling creates a few notable issues for the researcher: 1) What to use for data (i.e. which relevant population or populations to sample)?; and 2) When and how to disengage from the research project, or "theoretical saturation." For the process of theoretical sampling, data related to the research question are selected for comparison to generate common categories and shared properties. While making these selections, the researcher's goal is to identify and saturate these emergent categories, for the purpose of data-driven theoretical development (supported by the framework of saturated, emergent categories). Theoretical saturation has effectively been reached at the point in the data collection wherein additional observations and data collected among the selected population or populations are yielding no new insights into themes or categories relevant to the research question or sample population. When the point of theoretical saturation is achieved, the researcher disengages from theoretical sampling on the related category. This does not imply, however, that data collection is complete – just data collection on the category that has been effectively saturated. Further, Glasser (1978) warned that theoretical sampling is used not to justify and test "preconceived hypotheses" or verify theory, but to check and validate the emerging conceptual framework in progress. Moreover, the combined, continual use of theoretical sampling and the constant comparative method throughout the research process provides relatively stable checks and balance mechanisms to assist in producing final results that are actually grounded in the project data and well-planned. This research project adapts these methods as an effort to tease theoretical categories out of the gun stories and other project data, "weave the fractured story back together," and move the story told in a grounded theoretical direction (Glaser 1978:72 and Charmaz 2006: 63).

My fieldstudy on gun owners spanned a 3-year period, from January 2005 to January 2008. Field research included approximately 250 hours of direct interaction with research subjects in a variety of settings, including gun shows and live action play groups (e.g., "cowboy clubs"). In addition to field observations, a total of 52 semi-structured interviews (see interview schedule in appendix A) of varying length were conducted with a range of gun collectors and other gun owners in venues that included gun collectors' homes, different kinds of shooting events, and public gun shows throughout the Midwest. Further, the researcher has photographed gun collections and collected gun collectors' stories about the living histories of their individual guns. Contact was initiated face to face, at gun events, using a standardized approach script (see appendix D), and also via snowball sampling. For future researchers attempting to conduct similar research on gun culture, I feel that it is noteworthy to mention that although gun owners and enthusiasts are naturally guarded and trust can be quite difficult to establish, I found that I had much better success in terms of new contacts and questionnaire returns after I cut my hair off short and whenever my wife was in attendance with me.

Other data considered here include published materials circulated at gun shows (and other gun-related assemblies mentioned above), official data from the Bureau of Justice, gun culture websites, popular gun owner/collector publications, such as *The Official Gun Digest Book of Guns & Prices, The American Rifleman, Women and Guns, Guns and Ammo,* and popular song lyrics depicting gun imagery. Songs were selected as a relevant pop-culture aspect of gun data primarily based on the inescapable presence of gun-related song lyrics throughout this research process. Some of the identified themes pertaining to guns and gun use in popular culture are examined through the analysis of song lyrics depicting gun symbolism from various genres. Significant bodies of research exist that explore portrayals of gender symbolism in the media and advertisements (Carter and Steiner 2003; Vigorito and Curry 1998; Kirchler 1992), gender performance in music (Gottlieb and Wald 1994), guns as a source of symbolic empowerment (Jiobu and Curry 2001), and guns as a masculine power symbol (Brown 1994). Further, researchers have also documented "bifurcated" media portrayals of masculinity and femininity and called for "the exposure of cultural texts or symbolic meanings pertaining to gender by reviewing a variety of media" (Gottlieb and Wald 1994:252); however, representations of masculine expression of guns in music remain an unexplored area of social inquiry. Each area is considered in this research effort. Finally, pictures of some of the guns discussed are included. As most gun events are copyrighted and photos are not allowed to be taken, most image data from events appears in the form of handouts distributed at events.

As this research project came to a close, the investigator was pleasantly surprised, and somewhat vindicated to find that previous scholarly works such as *Interaction Ritual Chains* (2004) by Randall Collins had reached out to the scientific community, requesting work like mine, especially for the purposes of unraveling special qualities, mysteries and complications pertaining to guns and gun ownership.

DATA ANALYSIS

A general description of the data analysis used throughout this project is provided in this section. Note that to preserve the integrity and continuity of the grounded theory-based aspects of this project, additional, detailed analyses and specific findings of the data are also provided in the relevant sections of later chapters. Whenever possible, aspects of the data are explored as they unfolded during the active telling of gun stories and through direct, observed interactions with guns in their natural social environments. Charmaz (2006) characterizes the construction of grounded theory and related data analysis as a fluid, flexible, and an ongoing process. Glasser and Strauss (1967:65) indicate that for the collection and analyses of data, well-selected, often diversified slices of data, with essentially no limits as to the type or characteristics of the data are collected.

While the sociologist may use one technique of data collection primarily, theoretical sampling for saturation...allows a multi-faceted investigation, in which there are no limits to the techniques of data collection, the way they are used, or the types of data acquired. One reason for openness of inquiry is that…the sociologist works under the diverse structural conditions of each group: schedules, restricted areas, work tempos, the different perspectives of people in different positions, and the availability of documents of different kinds (65)

For the purpose of this research, to ensure that the data slices were as representative of gun culture as possible, all slices were carefully considered once embedded within pockets of gun culture, reviewed multiple times prior to beginning any coding, and discussed in detail with multiple study participants to carefully scrutinize "meanings." Also, consistent with the inductive nature of grounded theory, as opposed to a more typical "logico deductive" approach, I began analysis early on in the data collection process. More specifically, after settling on a research question and related data, I first began with an initial review of available gun data, allowing the unfolding data to guide the literature review, "sensitizing concepts and general disciplinary perspectives" (Charmaz 2006:11). This led to the identification of initial general concepts (overt and subtle), themes, and relationships among the data. Accordingly, initial data analysis began once the first events were attended and initial interviews were conducted. These initial discussions with research subjects and observations within gun culture settings were crucial to the process, as it served to guide future interview questions and conceptualization of the data.

As I worked through interviews and event data, emerging themes in the data were continually synthesized and analyzed to organize subsequent data collection and work toward an informed, grounded theory of the gun. As slices of data were collected in this area of inquiry, they were next informally coded and categorized within and across events and pieces of data, working toward saturation, as prescribed by Charmaz (2006). Accordingly, data collected at the events and interviews were reviewed several times prior to conducting any initial coding. Next, I utilized a crude form of line-by-line coding, thoroughly probing the text and attempting to isolate overt and latent "meaning." I refer to it as "crude," as much of the data has no obvious start or stop point that would indicate an obvious line of text (ex. much of the data exist in the form of pictures, decals, literatures, movie and song references, images of guns and sentence fragments). However, any specific detail from a piece of data that is distinct enough to communicate something obvious or specific makes it "stand alone" data, and constitutes a line for the purpose of this research.

A type of focused coding was then used to sort and synthesize the large amount of data collected by studying and comparing the initial codes. I sought out categories and themes that cut across venues and interviews. As directed by Glasser and Strauss (1967) and Charmaz (2006), for heightened rigor, attention to detail and accuracy, the constant comparative method was used throughout data analysis to make comparisons of responses between and among research subjects about similar aspects of the data following each interview and event.

The purpose of this qualitative analysis was to move toward a grounded theory of symbolic gun value within U.S. gun culture. Although many gun owners and collectors will describe the value of a gun based on special properties (such as serial number, unique design or limited availability) that give it a fixed and specific market or monetary value, borrowing from Durkheim (1965/1912), I am more interested in exploring the symbolic, emotional value that gun owners place on their guns. According to Durkheim (1965/1912), a vested emotional, symbolic value of an object or idea is a unique product of social interaction that centers around the concepts of respect and majesty. "To be sure, in the sentiment which the believer feels for the things he adores, there is always fear derived from respect and the dominating emotion of majesty" (79). By following the procedures outlined above, I seek to inquire as to what type of respect as well as awe or majesty-inspiring life experiences culminate in the formation of emotional attachment to firearms for gun owners and influence social interaction.

As an inductive process, grounded theory implies that no pre-conceived hypotheses are tested as an effort to validate the emergent theory. However, it is natural to the process to have certain hypotheses come into focus after the initial consideration of the data. These hypotheses may then be used to test emerging relationships between data and other data, categories/themes with other categories/themes, as well as between data and categories/themes. Accordingly, my eye toward the saturation of conceptual themes unfolding from this research project was partially guided by the following hypotheses that emerged from the initial wave of general data coding:

- The emotional value assigned to guns is fluid, not fixed, so it is contextually relevant

- Some guns will generate higher levels of emotional attachment than others

- Guns used in work (police) will have less emotional attachment than guns associated with leisure activities, especially those involving friends or family

- Guns that were used as part of some memorable activity, such as a hunt and kill will garner a higher emotional value than one that was merely purchased

- The greater the historical/social significance of a firearm, the greater the emotional attachment (ex. If it was handed down from a grandfather or parent, or owned by a renowned public figure, such as John Wayne)

- A firearm that was used as part of a rite of passage, such as being handed down from a family member to signify the transition into manhood, will garner a higher emotional value than a weapon of historical significance that is acquired from outside of the owner's primary social network

- The cost of a firearm has no relationship to the emotional attachment (outside of the presumed positive correlation between historical/social significance of a firearm and monetary value). Some of those most highly valued in a collection, eliciting the most emotional response will carry the lowest monetary or trade value

CREDIBILITY

In laying out the criteria for studies utilizing components of grounded theory, Glauser and Strauss (1967) and Charmaz (2006) each stresses the importance of establishing credibility with the study population as well as the audience reading the findings. Most of establishing credibility with the reading audience appears to hinge on the researcher's ability to provide details, details, details. The goal is to paint a vivid enough picture through thick description and data presentment to demonstrate believable "familiarity with the settings and topic" (Charmaz 2006:182). Toward this end of establishing credibility, I have included a substantial range of observations from numerous subjects, a variety of venues, and continually drawn comparisons among the data and settings. To establish credibility with my informants, continual efforts were made to remain engaging, respectful, genuinely interested, and to treat the work with them as a professional collaboration. In others words, I was sure to continually share my observations with the research subjects to ensure that they jibed with the stories they were providing, their intended meanings, and how the informants also interpreted various features at gun events that I have recounted.

Additional assurances of credibility were attempted through the use of a type of data auditing. Burton and Price-Spratlen (1999), introduced an issue with qualitative data collection that they called the contextual moment hypothesis. Their study revealed that even when a researcher is fortunate enough to have access to longitudinal data, sampling the same subjects on the meaning of identical items, over the course of several years, there is still as issue of concern relevant to data credibility. They demonstrated that a subject's perspective when providing an assessment about any type of value or feeling is subject to fluctuations throughout the day. A subject might answer the same survey instrument item differently, depending on aspects of the actual "contextual moment," such as neighborhood characteristics and life events that had unfolded on a given day. As my accurate accounts of project data are contingent on my attention to detail and successful transmission of shared meanings, in addition to the reliability of accounts supplied by the research subjects, the potential for fluctuations or inconsistencies in my informants' stories was a relevant concern. With these concerns in mind, I devised a form of data auditing suitable for this project.

First, as previously mentioned, I worked closely with informants to ensure that I accurately characterized stories and details that they shared. The auditing component created to ensure that informant accounts were not changing notably over time worked by contacting subjects who had provided detailed gun stories within 3 to 6 months of the time they provided their stories. By a combination of email, phone, fax and mail follow-ups (depending on the informant's preference), I provided accounts that were slightly different from the details given by the informants, changing minor details about their event descriptions, and omitting some of the key details, as well. I then compared the informants' comments/revisions to the original story details, checking for notable differences.

In the case of this project, the contextual moment did not prove to be an area of concern. The research subjects always caught the changes to story details and provided the original account again. Interestingly, it was only details pertaining to hunting that fluctuated a little, with subjects sometimes slightly altering the size of an animal killed with a gun. Accounts about why the owners valued a specific gun, or which guns they valued the most did not fluctuate. Whenever possible, in additions to descriptions of what I have observed, samples of the data in the form of detailed stories from informants, pictures of their guns, and copies of relevant event literature are included to help the reader understand the context more fully.

HUMAN SUBJECTS CONSIDERATION

As guns have proven to be a bit of a touchy subject among my informants, I was made aware very early on in the preliminary phases of this research that assurances of anonymity were a must. Prior to conducting any interviews, participants were ensured that I had no agenda other than to collect the stories of their guns. Each participant was provided a copy of a consent form (see Appendix B) prior to interviewing.

Initially, the project was designed to include the taping of subject interviews. However, during preliminary data collection, I noted that subjects were either turned off completely by taping, or just clammed up once the record button was pushed. I literally saw subjects begin to writhe in their chairs, and shift from being open fountains of information to providing only short/choppy responses. Witnessing this effect, I elected to suspend audio taping and rely on hand-written notes, other typed or hand-written accounts received directly from research subjects, and photographs.

As this research centers around values placed on guns, it was not necessary to photograph the owners with the guns. In addition to excluding subjects from photographs, I also used first names only on data collection materials, and in report findings, refer only to subjects as "respondent," "informant," or mention only a descriptive detail pertaining to their region or occupation. This serves the dual purpose of maintaining strict subject anonymity, while also simplifying coding and records management.

CHAPTER IV

Considering Pop Culture

"I think I'm beginning to understand all those gun/sex metaphors in songs and movies. After firing that thing, I'm pretty sure if I had a dick it would be hard right now." This comment was made by a female daycare teacher in the Midwest after firing an M-16 automatic rifle for the first time. She went on to add *"I enjoy shooting the handguns too, but the charge I got from this one was pure sex. I felt like such a badass. If I had been with my boyfriend he would have gotten so lucky afterwards. I would have been ready to jump him. There sure is a lot more going on there than just pulling trigger...shooting that thing... So exhilarating and hot."*

After working in this ongoing study for several years, I was aware that the respondent above was not imagining some of those sexual references to guns in various forms of popular culture. She also isn't alone in her feelings that sometimes there's more to firing a gun than just pulling the trigger. In addition to published academic literature on the topic of guns, I also reviewed magazines that targeted gun owners and users. There was, to say the least, no shortage of parallels made between gun use and ownership and various forms and degrees of sexual expression.

In order to gain a detailed understanding of guns, we must consider what is being said about guns and the information about guns being presented, whether text or image. Although extant research has documented separate media portrayals of masculinity and femininity in popular magazines and other forms of popular media (Carter and Steiner 2003; Vigorito and Curry 1998; Kirchler 1992) and called for "the exposure of cultural texts or symbolic meanings pertaining to gender by reviewing a variety of media" (Gottlieb and Wald 1994:252), gender representations of guns in popular magazines appear to be an unexplored area of social inquiry.

One participant probe used as part of the semi-structured research instrument was a consideration of gun-related publications frequently purchased or read by my informants. The two most commonly cited by my sample population were *Guns and Ammo*, and *American Rifleman*. A third publication that was mentioned by my informants, and also represented among popular publications displayed at attended events was *Women And Guns*. I included the third publication primarily for contrast, as well as diversity among target audiences. *Women and Guns* also serves as an interesting springboard into views that male gun owners appear to approve of and want shared with women.

While researching and writing this book, I regularly encountered back-dated issues of each of these publications. It is a common practice for gun show promoters and attendees to discard back-dated issues of gun-related literature at gun events, setting them out on display for review and giving them away to interested parties. Other issues were reviewed on newsstands around the greater Columbus, Ohio area.

A monthly publication *Guns and Ammo* caters to those who own, use, collect and have some active interest or love for firearms and all things firearms related. I also reviewed and obtained several past issues of *American Rifleman*, ranging in dates from the early 1980s to present. *American Rifleman* is a publication of the National Rifle Association (NRA). Finally, I reviewed hard copies of the publication *Women and Guns* at gun events and newsstands that dated back to the mid-1990s as well as articles listed in the online archive (May 2001 – April 2012). Also a monthly publication, *Women and Guns* is produced by the Second Amendment Foundation, which according to their website (www.saf.org) is a tax-exempt, non-profit, educational, research and publishing corporation.

Women and Guns is a convenient vantage point from which evaluate questions regarding the relationship between guns and gender performance– primarily the assertion I have made throughout this project that guns are objects of masculine definitions and social performances only via symbolic empowerment. Simple logic dictates that there is nothing inherently masculine or feminine about any inanimate object of form of material culture. Guns are no exception. A general firearm sales and educational publication, the magazine *Women and Guns* primarily targets a white, middle-class female demographic. After reviewing dozens of issues spanning 14 years, I also gleaned a clear presentation of a type of template demonstrating how, when and why women are to own and use guns. The very presence of this publication serves as notice that gun manufacturers recognize women owning guns in increasing numbers – and being worthy of a sales pitch. Logic dictates that this consideration only ever accompanies the acknowledgement of a potential market, buyer and likely sale.

Women and Guns also conveniently plays on the fear of crime, which has remained high in the past few decades (Zimring and Hawkins 1997), as well as the mass perception of a heightened need for protection for all of the women who spend time alone. While on the surface a gun culture push for greater diversity appears to have ushered in the publication of *Women and Guns*, upon further analysis, *Women and Guns* does not appear to challenge the traditional masculinities model of guns ownership in a notable way. I have observed in the magazine that women are usually accompanied by men, and often depicted as fearing men. Fear of victimization is continually appealed to as a type of advertising gimmick. Guns are most commonly presented as being needed primarily for the protection of women (women who needed to be protected from men, with the assistance from other men and GUNS!). The most typical scenarios of women using guns involves a need of a gun to protect them from, shadowy, lurking, criminal male stranger.

Interestingly, while females are far more likely to experience violence at the hands of acquaintances and significant others (Thio, Taylor and Schwartz 2012), I found no suggestion in the magazine that guns might be useful as a means of protection from others in the home, or perhaps partners or friends who do not cohabitate. Men were presented as both friends/protector and threats to women gun owners. Safe, friendly (white, middle class, fatherly and/or grandfatherly) men are depicted as teachers and companions to the female weapons owner. Unfriendly/dangerous men (minorities lurking in the shadows) are depicted as threats to women and one of the reasons that she needs the gun for protection. I should note that in the course of my magazine content analysis, I never encountered advertisements suggesting that the dangers facing women come in the form of abusive husbands, fathers, or anything other than the lurking, male creeper – presumably always a stranger.

American Rifleman is only available through the NRA. The subscription has long been included as one of two magazines as part of a membership with the NRA. Upon joining, members of the NRA are given a choice to receive either *American Rifleman* or *American Hunter* magazine. By far, *Guns and Ammo* has the most significant gun show presence and largest readership of the three magazines analyzed in this section. It is distributed via numerous outlets, including online, general newsstands and bookstores. *Women and Guns* is also available online, from newsstands and bookstores. It is, however, a bit more difficult to find. Throughout the course of this study, I found that local area grocery stores and also Barnes and Noble always carried *Guns and Ammo*, and I frequently found an issue or two of Women and Guns in these locations, as well. The magazines' availability varies widely in libraries. The Columbus Metropolitan Library carries sporadic issues of *Guns and Ammo* from 1958 to present, but not *Women and Guns*. The Athens, Ohio Public Libraries, however, carries mixed issues of each. A librarian at the Columbus Public Library explained to me, however, that it is not always the national volume of sales that determines what they have on the shelves. Subscription/publication availability is also determined, in part, by the active interest of patrons and librarians, as well as donations.

The most interesting location where I found copies of *Guns and Ammo* is Port Columbus International Airport. It just never occurred to me that airplanes and guns were a reasonable or expected combination. The other two publications, however, were not available at the airport. I have not found either magazine to be commonly circulated in University libraries.

Each of the magazines frequently depicts a variety of guns, ammunition, auxiliary items, political statements (contradictory positions on the government, calling for a need for guaranteed protection of constitutional rights – primarily the 2nd Amendment – and shouting loudly about fear of the perversions and tyrannical motives of government agents) and services and related sales pitches. Guns are depicted in the cover art, the stories and advertisements running throughout and included in the end matter. Guns are depicted by themselves, much as if they were a celebrity in some popular culture magazine. After pouring over every detail of dozens of like magazines, the guns and associated products seem commonplace – as expected as what you might find flipping through a J.C. Penney's Catalog. I have noticed while collecting project data that whether they are physically present or depicted in photographs or some other form of media, guns generally seem to stand out, catch and hold the viewers' attention. I observed the same to be true on the homes of most informants. They know that guns are dangerous, frequently valuable and sometimes even shocking to unexpectedly see in plain view. In kind, there's a culture of courtesy and safety surrounding gun ownership. Most owners comply and keep at least the bulk of their firearms concealed, locked away or carefully hidden.

Gun safety, community awareness and educational literature published and distributed at gun events by both the NRA and PRO commonly depict families interacting in home environments without including guns in the photos at all. However, the typical magazine advertisement depictions of guns everywhere does suggest that guns are commonplace, not to be feared (when in the hands of the good guys) or hidden. Instead, they are everywhere and "safe." Another message promoted through the saturation style display of guns is that the presence of guns is as natural as breathing and not really so different than the family photo album, remote control or umbrella stand. Other items frequently normalized in these publications are those which are, in many states, illegal to buy, sell or own.

True to its name, *Woman and Guns* attempts to not only normalize guns in the lives of some women (mostly white and middle class), at least to a point, it seeks to empower them. The images are not just of women with guns. These are modern women. Women in the know. Women learning about guns the right way (i.e. most likely from the men in their lives). While the publication clearly seeks to education female subscribers about guns while selling their products, the message comes through pretty clearly that guns are not as natural to women as they are men; and, unlike men, women have a definitive need to be far-more heavily trained in the wise ways of manly guns.

Increasingly more military-style weapons, and often several at a time are featured on these magazine covers. Without exception, all of the magazines freely depict gun owners and users with guns in their hands, actively using or preparing to use gun. This serves as a constant reminder that these guns are intended for a utilitarian purpose, and meant to be discharged – always by humans, and sometimes AT humans. As previously mentioned, women are often portrayed in the same photos of men, but with males serving as a supervisor and/or instructor. The women are typically holding guns in some sort of student or amateur capacity. Again, the messages here is pretty loud and clear that this process just isn't quite natural to women – not just because they are students, but because they are women. From this perspective, women are portrayed not only as naturally needing guidance in the process of gun handling, but specifically guidance from males who know the process intuitively. The dominant message is that women in guns and life are dependent on men.

Sexuality is a common, recurring theme in each publication. For example several issues of *Guns and Ammo* featured an article on shotgun barrel length with the ad text asserting "Shotgun barrel length. The vote is in...longer is better!" The sexual connotations are blatant. In the worlds of guns and sex, size matters, so GO BIG!. Would be buyer, the size of the barrel just might say something about the size of your penis and/or virility. In advertisements common to *Women and Guns*, size still matters, but the message is about the value of going compact. Concealment can save your life. And why not? For female buyers, there's no real concern for challenging their masculinity.

What appears to be happening is that weapons and ammunition manufacturers have been tasked with selling a product line long associated almost exclusively with men and masculinity. As a result of having to recreate the audience base (to tap into the other 50% of the population and consumers of goods), women have been creatively re-informed or re-socialized to perceive a want and need for something for which they historically had no (or little expressed) interest. The marketing schemes must be working, at least to a point. It is currently estimated that as many as fifteen to twenty million women, or 1 in every 10 women own guns in the United States (General Social Survey 2011).

It isn't just marketing and advertising in gun-related trade publications that have rapidly evolved to normalize female gun use and ownership. While guns are still identified with men and masculinity, with men owning 90% or more of known firearms, millions of women own their own guns too (McCrum 2011). In her (2011) book *Chicks With Guns*, Lindsay McCrum, using pictorial layouts, depicted female gun owners in a variety of settings, with guns appearing as a natural part of their background and landscape. The logic was sound. With several million women in the United States living with and around guns, for many of them, those who are not griped with fear or unaccustomed to handling firearms, the guns are genuinely a normal part of their life and environment. Part of the motivation behind the project was to dispel the notion among the general population that guns and women do not go together.

These magazines and other forms of media, such as the McCrumen book mentioned above, offer a way for men and women to (re)define and (re)construct gun related behavior along gender, racial, and political lines. Gun use and ownership is a way for people to express themselves in sport as well as the added bonus of self protection. Guns allow users to maintain a way of life in which men and women can participate in self expression and proactively protect against trespasses and intrusions. The guns also offer a semi-paradoxical political platform for many. A contradictory stance is taken in regard to the role of and confidence in the state. While the magazines staunchly proclaim that government interference is unwanted in gun control, understood as regulating access to guns, they want the state to maintain and protect the right to own guns. By portraying guns as properly controlled by men and gun behavior as one expression of masculinity, these popular magazines focus attention on the meaning of guns as arising from the interactions among gender-performing people and guns. Simply stated, the images depicted by the magazines, pertaining to guns, may then be incorporated and re-incorporated into gendered-performances surrounding the perceived meaning, use and owning of guns as a symbolically charged piece of culture.

What is commonly missing in these magazines, based on my extended observations, is the much-needed focus on the victimization of women at the hands of those in their own homes and known to them, and not some shadowy stranger. Similarly, the publications aimed at men do not address the real threat of men using guns to inflict violence against others as some socially-reinforced, symbolic masculine gesture. Towards this end, the marketing efforts and educational and training efforts of these publications have roundly failed.

GUNS AND MUSIC

One of the more interesting and surprising caveats to this research has been the intersection of gun symbolism and popular music - an area that has yet to be explored scientifically. Guns as a source of symbolic empowerment have been established by Jiobu and Curry (2001), and Brown (1994) demonstrated the use of guns as a masculine power symbol. Recent research on gender dynamics in music has depicted separate gender performances for males and females pertaining to the playing, writing, performing and sharing of music, with unequal access to music-related symbols portrayed as the most masculine (Leonard 2007; Darling-Wolf 2004; Whiteley 1997; Gottlieb and Wald 1994). There also appears to be a gender order in music that is well-regulated to preserve existing patriarchal structures (Leonard 2007; Whiteley 1997). Masculine expressions of guns in music, however, were first explored as a scientific research area by Taylor (2009).

Throughout every phase of this project, I have been unable to escape music references to guns. It began while gathering data at the first gun show that I attended – even though I didn't know it. T-shirts and bumper stickers displayed the saying "happiness is a warm machine gun." A few months later, while conducting field research at a cowboy club tournament, I was watching a female shooter who, upon finishing her shooting event, turned and walked over to a large man standing directly behind her, fully adorned in cowboy apparel. With a very large smile on her face, appearing to beam with self-satisfaction, she looked at him and said "happiness is a warm gun…bang, bang…shoot, shoot…" At the time, I thought the tournament participant was making a turn of phrase. It was not until later, when performing word searches on music lyric data bases that I realized this all-too-common expression in the world of guns has its origins in what I considered to be the unlikeliest place of all: it stems from a Beatles song from *The White Album*, on a track titled simply "Happiness is a Warm Gun." I was a bit surprised by this song's visible impact on the gun world, given the Beatles well-publicized association with the peace movement and the not-so-subtle irony that John Lennon was killed by a deranged man with a pistol. It was not the revelation that this popular phrase was actually part of a Beatles song that caused me to notice the heavy emphasis on guns in contemporary music lyrics, however. Much of what I noticed was in retrospect.

As with any research adventure that requires the principle researcher to be submersed in the subject of study, I naturally became sensitized as to the overall presence of my subject matter in society at large – I probably saw it popping up in places where I would have previously not noticed. Take t-shirts and bumper stickers for instance. After seeing popular slogans sold and warn by participants at a variety of gun events, I began to notice them everywhere I went. Although this will be covered in more detail later, as it is relevant to topic sensitization, a sampling of some of the more interesting are as follows:

9 out of the 10 voices in my head told me to stay home and CLEAN the guns

Gun Control Means Hitting Your Target

In Glock I Trust

Why Yes, I Do Shoot Like A Girl

Up Your Arsenal

Gun Control Means Never Having To Say I Missed You

The First Rule of Gun Safety: Don't Piss Me Off

Guns Are Great, Guns Are Good, Let Us Thank Them For Our Freedom. Amen

More surprising than the volume of gun symbols on t-shirts, was the presence of gun-related publications at book stores, newsstands and grocery stores. Throughout the course of this study, I found that local area grocery stores and also Barnes and Noble always carried *Guns and Ammo*, and I frequently found an issue or two of *Women and Guns* in these locations, as well. One participant probe used as part of the semi-structured research instrument was a consideration of gun-related publications frequently purchased or read by my informants. The two most commonly cited by my sample population were *Guns and Ammo*, and *American Rifleman*. A third publication that was mentioned by my informants and also represented among popular publications displayed at attended events was *Women And Guns*.

The magazines' availability varies widely in libraries. The Columbus Metropolitan Library carries sporadic issues of *Guns and Ammo* from 1958 to present, but not *Women and Guns*. The Athens,

Ohio Public Libraries, however, carries mixed issues of each. A librarian at the Columbus Public Library explained to me, however, that it is not always the national volume of sales that determines what they have on the shelves. Subscription/publication availability is also determined, in part, by the active interest of patrons and librarians, as well as donations.

But it was while driving to one of my first gun events that I noticed as I flipped through local radio stations on a 30-minute drive, that several of the songs referenced guns. One was the Jim Croce song "Leroy Brown," stating that Leroy had a ".32 gun in his pocket for fun." I had probably heard the song hundreds of times growing up, and the line about the gun for fun never really stood out. On the same trip, I also came across the song "Saturday Night Special," by Leonard Skynard. I discovered through the course of my gun research, that the .32 gun referenced in the classic Jim Croce tune is actually the same as the "Saturday Night Special" mentioned by Leonard Skynard. According to their song about this infamous gun, "it's got a barrel that's blue and cold. Ain't good for nothing, but put a man six feet in a hole..." Yet another song I came across while flipping through radio stations, "Pumped up Kicks" by Foster the People broached the topic of teen angst and guns through humor, through the warning of one teen to his peers that they had better "outrun" his gun and run "faster" than his bullet. Each of these songs speaks to separate themes common in the world of the gun, and these are fun and fear, respectively. Once this connection was revealed, and it became clear that the overt gun references were endemic in contemporary music lyrics, at least a general analysis seemed appropriate, if not necessary.

Gun Lyric Sources

In addition to noting convenient references to guns as I encountered them on the radio, I found that there is actually a variety of large music lyric data bases available at no charge to the general public. Before getting into details about these data bases and the searches performed, I think it worthwhile to demonstrate that data do, indeed, sometimes come from the unlikeliest of sources. I doubt that I am unique as a researcher, in that, at times, I struggled desperately to locate sources or slices of data that epitomized the message that I intend to convey. In the winter of 2007, I stumbled across one such source, in the form of a song from the popular country music iconoclast Toby Keith. The song is titled "Love Me If You Can," and it includes the simple lyric "My father gave me my shotgun that I'll hand down to my son, try to teach him everything it means." It bothered me for days that this simple one-liner said so much about what I am trying to reveal about gun symbolism through this research – and, in some ways, with a far-more tidy summary than I could accomplish with several paragraphs of text. I want to know "everything it means" to the man passing along a gun to his son. By collecting these gun stories and asking people to share the stories of their guns, and what each gun means to them, I want to know what Toby is claiming to already know.

Toward this end of understanding the meaning of guns and how we use them to interact, I found myself perusing large song lyric data bases. My two primary search engines housed very large collections. The first is elyrics.net, which houses lyrics to almost 154,000 songs ranging from pop and rock to rap and country. I liked this search engine because it allows the user to perform keyword searches on both song titles and song text. Using the word "pistol" alone, I found 747 songs referencing the word "pistol," and another 123 songs referencing the word "guns." There are more songs that include references to specific guns by caliber, such as 9mm and .357, as well. My other preferred music lyric data base was cowboylyrics.com. From this site, keyword searches can also be performed. A simple keyword search pulled up 2398 songs that use the word gun either in the title or song text, and another 883 referencing pistols. At a glance, my initial reaction was there's no way that guns are referenced in that many songs. Naturally, some of the gun and pistol references were metaphorical, and often in reference to the male sex organ, such as the case in the famous late 1970s rock anthem "Love Gun," by the band Kiss in which an overtly amorous young man celebrates the object of his affection who has "pulled the trigger" of his "love gun." After spending considerable time reviewing the song lists, I quickly became aware that themes of the songs mirrored the popular themes noted in the gun research as well as those unfolding from my own project data. As referenced in the story lines and sampling of the lyrics below, to be sure, some of the songs were, indeed, accounts of gratuitous violence. I found examples of these in multiple genres, including country, rap/hip-hop, rock and punk.

In the popular rock song Santeria, by Sublime, for instance, a character named Sanchito is being warned to run and hide if he knows what's good for him, because

> Daddy's got a new.45 and I won't think twice to stick that
> barrel straight down Sancho's fucking throat.

We find a very similar style of story-telling pertaining to the gun use in the song Delia's Gone, as performed by well-known country and popular music icon Johnny Cash. In this song, a story is relayed from the perspective of a man chatting with his jailer about the ghost of his former love "Delia," who haunts his dreams. He provides explicit and gruesome details about how and why he shot the "cold," "mean," "low down," and "triflin'" woman with his submachine gun.

> First time I shot her, I shot her in the side…
> Hard to watch her suffer, but with the second shot she died…

The theme of retaliatory violence for some sort of perceived personal trespass via gun use is not uncommon to rap/hip-hop music. As an effort to describe prevalent neighborhood conditions and facts of urban gang life, modern day street poets such as Snoop Dog and Lil' Wayne paint visual portraits of the reality of gun violence in their social worlds, through their words and rhymes. As expressed by Snoop Dog in his "Ghetto Symphony"

> I pop a cap in yo' ass…Man fuck all that yappin'…
> We 'bout that gun clappin'…

Lil' Wayne is even more descriptive about gang violence and gun use, supplying the when and why to use them in his song "Wish You Would." He describes a situation in which his family has been victimized by some non-specific group. Now, if they cross him again, he will lash out with extreme justice, with "ghetto justice," by "raining bullets" on their families. As he states

> Let's get the pistols out the trunk…Leave a nigga block full of
> nothin' but guts, brains…You bet' not play with me cause I
> cock my gun …

References to guns for committing acts of violence like these were fairly typical across rock, country, punk and rap genres. However, there were also non-violent themes typical to gun culture, such as the *badass factor* and *masculinity* of guns, guns as a *comedic prop*, and guns as a *site of rituals*. The final theme that I noted pertained to women and guns. Whereas gun lyrics pertaining to men may be used to display power, ritual or entertainment, gun lyrics involving women invariably portray women as victims. They are either using guns to protect themselves or to lash out against someone who has hurt them. Even in song lyrics, the masculine center of guns is highly protected. In using guns in songs, women are not only relegated to a second-class citizen and victim, but they are also not portrayed as trading on the "badassedness" or "badassitudes" of the gun. The following section includes a sampling of popular gun themes and lyrics to illustrate my point.

GUNS: THE BADASS/MASCULINITY FACTOR

Somehow, it almost seems rude to have a scholarly discussion about the badass and masculine factor of guns without leading off with a focus on *"Folsom Prison Blues,"* by the late Johnny Cash. The line "when I was just a baby, my mama told me son, always be a good boy, don't ever play with guns" speaks volumes about how guns are perceived by many males in contemporary U.S. society. Playing with guns makes you a "bad boy." The concept of being "bad" is very rock & roll, and often portrayed as desirable to the type of women who men are supposed to want to attract. Another line in the song which helps to illuminate the masculine power imbued in guns is the classic line "I shot a man in Reno, just to watch him die." Although this image is one of undeniable, gratuitous violence, it is also one of absolute power. Here the gun is the ultimate symbol of hyper masculinity. The "bad boy" has taken a gun, empowered himself and, for an instant, was master of someone else's fate.

In the song "I'm Still a Guy," by Brad Paisley, we find a slightly different approach to protecting the masculine center of guns in popular music. Although there is technically a heavy comedic feel to this song, the use of the gun is an interesting study in masculine capital and symbolic empowerment. Here we have a man lamenting that he doesn't want to be neutered by carrying his girlfriend's purse or walking her sissy, little dog. How does he retain his "pair," (of testicles/balls) given his plight? Interestingly, the writer references guns not only in the last line of the song to secure his manhood,

> Oh my eyebrows ain't plucked, there's a gun in my truck
> Oh thank God, I'm still a guy

he also opens the song with a line about shooting animals. He has "symbolically empowered" himself with guns as a masculine power symbol as a direct response to the affront to his masculinity. The song begins with commentary about a trophy deer kill (Bambi) hanging on his wall – or at least that's where he feels that a deer belongs, as opposed to his girlfriend's view of deer in a more peaceable sense.

Many of the songs of troubadour Marty Robbins mentioned guns and described their use in a very elaborate western movie, picturesque manner. He was a master of using a song to characterize a duel to the death with guns. Typical of his repertoire was the song "Big Iron," which chronicled an Arizona Ranger's pursuit of an outlaw named "Texas Red." He had tracked him down, sworn to bring him in "alive or maybe dead." The ranger called Texas Red out into the streets and then went to work with "the big iron on his hip." As the song unfolds, the outlaw was a ruthless killer, but he was no match for the Arizona Ranger that day.

> Texas Red had not cleared leather 'fore a bullet fairly ripped
> And the Ranger's aim was deadly with the big iron on his hip.

In this song, it is difficult to escape the true "cowboy cool" just dripping from the imagery. When he sings of the cowboy ready to "do some business with the big iron on his hip," we might as well be watching Clint Eastwood in an all-too familiar scene with a cigar tightly clinched between his teeth. This cowboy is brave, tough, and definitely performing with his gun the "right way." This aspect of "badassedness," or type of cool surrounding guns and gun use permeates every aspect of gun culture that I have had the opportunity to observe while conducting my extensive field research. Something similar to the scene depicted in this song is a close approximation to what many of my informants recounted as the dream they are chasing when they hold their favorite guns – and sometimes slip them into their cowboy holsters. As one of my research subjects so eloquently stated: "Sometimes, when it comes to the male fascination with guns, it's as simple as John Wayne, the Lone Ranger, Gene Autry and other matinee heroes."

GUN AS HIGH COMEDY?

In general, guns are serious subject matter, and there's nothing particularly funny about them at all. However, while researching the music lyric data bases, I came across several popular songs that do use guns as a type of comedic prop. This could either be to make guns appear less dangerous by making light of their awful power, or simply because sometimes it's easier to laugh about the things that we fear the most (to sort of reclaim the power they hold over us).

The first comedic gun ballad that I encountered was a #1 hit for country music singer Mark Chestnut titled "Bubba Shot the Jukebox." In this song, poor Bubba has had his heart broken, and decided to take his pain out on the jukebox by shooting it. Or as the song goes, he decided to pull his gun and shoot the jukebox in retaliation for a song that was played on it that made him cry.

> Went to his truck and got a forty five
> Bubba shot the juke box last night

Country and popular music performer Al Dexter sang a couple of gun-related songs with comedic themes. The first, a song titled "Run Red Run," depicts an altercation between a poker player named Red, and his monkey. The owner teaches the monkey to drink beer and play poker; and, unfortunately for red, the monkey is a sore loser at cards. Red finds himself staring down the barrel of his own gun, with the monkey on the other end.

> The monkey said Red you made a man out of me, now I'm going to make a monkey out of you.

Another of Al Dexter's songs, "Pistol Packin' Mama,", relates the tale of a husband who likes to drink and party far more than his wife is willing to tolerate. After catching Al out on the town with another woman, she pulls a pistol and kills them both.

Now there was old Al Dexter - he always had his fun
But with some lead, she shot him dead - his honkin' days are
done.

This song is an interesting mixture of themes. First, we are definitely supposed to find it funny that the lead character in the song is chased around by a violent women wielding a pistol. However, true to the formula of women in songs with guns, this is not a simple issue of a woman symbolically empowering herself with a gun. Once again, we are supposed to believe that in response to what a man has repeatedly done to a woman – in the form of habitual maltreatment, she has, at long last, resorted to violence and the use of the gun as an equalizer.

GUNS AS A RITUAL SITE

Emile Durkheim established the standard for studying ritual behavior with his (1965/1912) *Elementary Forms of the Religious Life*. Durkheim perceived rituals as both "determined modes of action" (51) and "rules of conduct which prescribe how a man should comport himself in the presence of sacred objects" (56). According to Turner (2000) and Goffman (1967), at our current state of social evolution, it is impossible for human social interaction to exist without the assistance of interaction rituals. Rituals, which are typically "emotion-arousing," are used to begin and end all interactions, and also set the stage for everything that occurs socially in between (Turner 2000). Goffman (1967) expanded on Durkheim's sacred-centric definition of rituals, adding that rituals "represent ways in which the individual must guard and design the symbolic implications of his acts while in the immediate presence of an object that has a special value for him" (57). As Birrell (1981) noted, this expanded definition broadens the application value of rituals as a site of social observations, in that it is not limited to rare subject matter that is set aside as sacred.

Guns make for an interesting case study, in that they make it difficult for the researcher to disentangle the Durkheim from the Goffman. In other words, some of the gun owners clearly depict their guns as sacred objects that are "awe inspiring," and something to be set aside and revered. Others gun owners, however, lean far more toward Goffman's point of view, describing their guns as important, meaningful and "special," but by no means on the same level as an authentic object of religious worship. Whether depicted as "sacred" or simply "special and meaningful," the world of the gun is rich with ritual activity surrounding their use.

The Toby Keith song that was referenced at the start of this section titled "Love Me If You Can" hints to the deep symbolic meaning of guns, and a type of ritual-like activity surrounding the owning and passing down of guns. From the line "my father gave me my shotgun that I'll hand down to my son, try to teach him everything it means," we can see that there is much more than valuable property being exchanged. The singer is referencing a code and an entire way of life, the meanings of which are all tied up in the ceremonial passing on of this gun.

One type of gun-related ritual that came up several times during the course of this project involved gun cleaning. Although this will be detailed in a later section, it is very common for gun owners to have a special type of cleaning ritual for guns they value the most (not just monetarily, but more typically for sentimental reasons). However, a few of my informants also regaled me with accounts of another special kind of gun cleaning ritual. Among some gun owners who have daughters of dating age, it has become a type of half-serious/half-joking ritual to have the would-be unfortunate male suitor presented to meet the girl's father while he (the father) is in the process of cleaning one of his guns. While conducting this cleaning exercise, the father is laying down all the rules and expectations about how he expects his daughter to be treated. I found this type of account to be played out in a song currently in the top 10 of the country music charts titled "Cleaning This Gun," by Rodney Atkins. The general sentiment of the song is manifest in the following lines:

> I'll see you when you get back
> Bet I'll be up all night still cleaning this gun

PROTECTING THE MASCULINE CENTER OF GUNS IN MUSIC

Song lyric references about females with guns are not rare. However, as I observed with popular gun magazines, and among attendees and a variety of gun events, women with guns are subjected to a patriarchy-based power struggle even in song. First, unlike men, women were not portrayed in any of the songs I reviewed as using guns just for fun. It also appears that the badassitudes enjoyed by men who usurp the symbolic power of the gun as part of their gender performance does not translate into song lyrics – at least not in an obvious way. Even when the song is about a female who is wielding her gun, it is invariably because she has been victimized in some way. It is almost as if the songwriters go out of their way to ensure that the image portrayed is not just a female who is tough, bad, and wielding a gun for no reason – and never like Johnny Cash's "Folsom Prison Blues," wherein the song's main character has shot a man "just to watch him die." One of the most detailed songs that I have encountered to illustrate this point is Aerosmith's "Janie's Got A Gun." This song is the prototypical scenario of a woman with a gun, who kills a man (her father), but only after years of systematic sexual abuse. Not only is there a history of sexual abuse, but no one that she tells believes that her father is guilty of anything. As the song goes, not only did Janie get a gun, she "put a bullet in his brain."

> What did her daddy do? He touched a little bitty baby - the man has got to be insane

Upon the initial review, another song that is currently at the top of the country music charts, "Gunpowder and Lead," by Miranda Lambert sounds almost additudinal enough to cash in on traditional masculine badassitudes ascribed to gun use in songs. Here vocals are edgy and direct, and she almost pulls it off. Additionally, the singer is insisting that good little girls are made not of "sugar and spice," as the old adage goes, but "gun powder and lead."

Close analysis of the lyrics reveal, however, the familiar plight of a woman who was pushed too far. She's not just a bad girl for the sake of being a bad girl, or a girl packing heat just because she likes guns. This is more of an account of a woman who is tired of being "slapped" and shaken "like a rag doll." Her significant other is on his way home from jail (presumably for spousal abuse). In anticipation of his return, the woman who is the focal point of the story has put together a little surprise party, and is laying in wait with a loaded shotgun.

> His fist is big but my gun's bigger
> He'll find out when I pull the trigger

Once again, similar to the female victim mentioned in the last set of lyrics, systematic abuse is revealed. Instead of the bad girl that the singer appears to be depicting through her forceful and powerful vocal delivery, what we actually have is a woman driven to the gun by a man who has repeatedly "shaken her like a rag doll," "slapped her face," and pounded her with his "fist." Although my lyrics review was far from comprehensive in the rock, country and rap genres, and it is possible that song lyrics exist that promote the truly empowered, badass woman, it is not what I found. Instead, I found evidence of a type of template-like, controlled gun use scenarios for women, much like what was observed in the field and through popular literature. In other words, much like what was found with the gradual empowerment of women in gun-related magazine publications, there appears to be a lingering resistance to placing women in the full masculine center of guns in music. The rules are still slightly different. While discussing this observation with one of my informants, she suggested that the song "The Night the Lights Went Out in Georgia," by Vicki Lawrence, does, in fact, portray a woman taking up a gun and shooting a man not because she was a victim, but because her brother was victimized.

However, there is one fatal flaw with stating that the female, gun wielding character in this classic song was enjoying true gun-related badassedness. It is true that the line "Little sister don't miss when she aims her gun" does sound like real "cowboy cool." The failure to cash in on the cowboy cool factor is that although she does shoot and kill someone (not to defend herself, but to protect her brother's honor – the stuff "real men" are made of), she ultimately does it in a cowardly fashion. The song ends with the woman's brother being hung for the crime that she had committed – and she never comes forward. True badass cowboys would never let someone else take the fall for their crimes, and they feel no need to hide from their gun use. Instead, they take to the gun as something as natural as breathing. It is a well-established form of legitimate, masculine currency.

In the end, this scenario reminded me of one of the scenes in the Gary Cooper classic "High Noon." The female character played by Grace Kelly is the only woman who ever touches a gun in the movie. Although she ultimately takes up arms to defend her husband and not herself, the way in which her gun use plays out keeps her from claiming any legitimate masculine capital or badassedness from her actions. She shoots an armed man in the only way that every self-

respecting cowboy knows you cannot: she shoots him in the back.
This movie example is over fifty years old; notwithstanding, much of
the symbolism pertaining to women and guns depicted in this scene
resonates in the words of Browder (2006), whose research findings
indicate that "in the American imagination, the armed woman will
continue to confound, arouse, and scare us" (232).

CHAPTER V

A Day at The Gun Event

"Alright Mary, you get her to look at the cookbooks while I show this gentleman some hardware. They look like they're here to spend." This comment was made by a vendor to his wife and partner at a Berea, Ohio guns how.

The following section chronicles typical findings at Ohio-area gun shows and shooting events visited from January 2005 to January 2008. The largest gun show in the southwest, which was hosted in Tyler, TX, was also attended to demonstrate theoretical saturation – this was covered in detail in the methods section. The primary purpose of visiting a variety of gun-related events was to make contact with potential research subjects and gain admission into the world of guns. The secondary purpose of this study was to gather enough gun-related data to identify recognizable patterns or categories of interaction pertaining to guns, gun symbolic values and gun use within the context of gun events – and work toward saturation of those theoretical categories. These categories, once identified, will help work toward grounded theory to illuminate specific ways in which guns and their symbolic values might influence gun-related interactions and behavior.

Although gun shows have received little attention from the academic community, this research expands on two previous studies that have unearthed separate aspects of gun shows and their significance. The first notable study was conducted by Stenross (1994), in which she described the business aspects of the gun show, from the perspective of the vendor and collector, and how they go about integrating guns and legitimate business, albeit for different reasons (i.e. instant profit for the vendor, and possible long-term investment or sentimental value for the collector). The second notable contribution in this area comes in the form of a (1999) report issued by the Bureau of Alcohol, Tobacco, Firearms and Explosives (ATF), wherein detailed descriptions of the types of activities, products and services encountered at gun shows throughout the U.S. were cataloged. To date, however, no research study has offered a thick, descriptive analysis of the symbolism and symbolic interaction surrounding gun culture. The findings reveal that guns have transcended their simple utility as a mechanism for discharging bullets, or in some cases, pieces of collectible art, and are used to facilitate a variety of social processes and interactions.

Guns in the U.S. are big business, and they are all around us. As indicated by a January 29, 2008 report issued by the Bureau of Alcohol, Tobacco, Firearms and Explosives (referred to from this point on as the ATF), in the year 2006, 1,403,329 handguns, 1,496,505 rifles, 714,618 shotguns and 35,872 "miscellaneous other firearms were manufactured in the U.S. (See table 5.1).

Not including guns that are exported, this total comes to approximately 3,282,803 new guns in U.S. circulation per year. This is just one year's production totals. A 1995 ATF report revealed that in the range of years from 1899 to 1993, more than 223 million guns were produced for sale and distribution in the United States. This estimate does not include the unknown quantity of additional firearms that were either seized, destroyed or lost. According to U.S. census population estimates, the U.S. population at the end of 1993 was approximately 259 million – indicating that there were enough guns in circulation to arm about 95% of the population, including infants, with at least one gun. Using these crude production estimates, by 2008, there are approximately 272,242,045 guns at large in the U.S. At this high volume, the exact number is irrelevant for the purpose of this study, as the quantity has far exceeded the point at which the presence of guns is recognizable and felt – half of this amount would still be a very large number. A (2006:1752) international comparative study conducted by Gross, Killias,Urs-Hepp, Gadola, Bopp,Christoph-Lauber, Schnyder, Gutzwiller and Rossler lists the U.S. high atop the list of nations with households reporting a high proportion of gun ownership (see table 5.2). The data reveal that U.S. households are more than twice as likely to own firearms as households in Canada or France, four times more likely than Australia, more than ten times as likely as England, Wales or Scotland, and more than forty times more likely than Japan.

Although these raw data do not take individual national histories and cultural differences into account, it is no less revealing about the heightened presence of guns in the U.S.

Table 5.1: U.S. Firearm Production by type, 2006

2006 FIREARMS MANUFACTURING REPORT

GUNS MANUFACTURED

PISTOLS		REVOLVERS	
Caliber	Total	Caliber	Total
.22	141,651	.22	84,452
.25	9,625	.32	2,242
.32	39,197	.357 MAG	99,562
.380	126,939	.38 SPEC	85,321
9MM	352,383	.44 MAG	54,308
.50	351,465	.50	56,184
Total	1,021,260	Total	382,069

RIFLES	1,496,505
SHOTGUNS	714,618
MISC.	35,872

GUNS EXPORTED

PISTOLS	144,779
REVOLVERS	28,120
RIFLES	102,829
SHOTGUNS	57,771
MISC.	34,022

Adapted from a January, 2008 report from the Bureau of Alcohol, Tobacco, Firearms and Explosives. Retrieved on March 15, 2008 from http://www.atf.treas.gov/firearms/stats/afmer/afmer2006.pdf

Table 5.2: Proportion of Households Owning Firearms, by Country in the Year 2000

Country	Proportion of Households with Firearms
United States	40.0
France	18.6
Canada	19.1
Australia	10.0
England and Wales	3.4
Scotland	3.3
Japan	0.6

Adapted from Ajdacic-Gross et al. 2006. "Changing Times: A Longitudinal Analysis of International Firearm Suicide Data." American Journal of Public Health. 96(10):1752-1754.

Why so many guns? In addition to previously discussed contributing factors such as fear (Zimring and Hawkins 1997) and lack of confidence in the Government and its ability to protect (Jiobu and Curry 2001), another possibility is the extremely attractive bottom line. Hoovers Inc., a company dedicated to informing consumers about revenues generated by each industry reports that the U.S. firearms industry is comprised of about 200 companies. These companies reported a combined annual revenue of over two billion dollars:

> The largest gun manufacturers are Remington Arms and Sturm Ruger. Other companies that manufacture more than 50,000 weapons annually are Marlin Firearms, Mossberg, Smith & Wesson, US Repeating Arms, Savage Sports Corporation, Beretta, and Hi-Point. Winchester Ammunition and Remington are major manufacturers of ammunition... Demand, which has been flat for years, is partly driven by hunters and partly by weapon upgrades by police departments. The profitability of individual companies is closely linked to marketing. Small companies can compete effectively by producing premium-priced high-quality or decorative guns.

Although automation has increased, the industry is still fairly labor-intensive: average annual revenue per worker is about £150,000" (Hoovers Inc., 2008).

However, the attractive profits gained by those selling firearms do not reveal anything about the appeal for the buyers/owners. It is clear that there are a lot of guns in circulation - some for sport, some for protection, and some for other reasons to be explored. In this section, I venture into an often controversial arena of the gun that has not been widely explored, although it is an area well known to gun owners: gun shows. As interactions and symbolic meaning pertaining to guns are a central focus of this research, gun shows offered one clear vantage point from which to observe interaction with firearms on a mass scale, in addition to presenting a research population with gun stories to share.

According to a report issued by the ATF in June, 2007, each year, the Bureau of Alcohol, Tobacco, Firearms and Explosives investigates gun shows and operations in an attempt to control the illegal selling of guns. The report reveals more than 4,000 gun shows are held each year in the United States (ATF 2007; ATF 1999:1). These gun exhibitions are a place where licensed and private sellers are able to advertise their products to known users. They also serve as a venue where guns, ammunition, gun parts, gun accessories and literature, may be sold, traded and discussed. The Bureau indicates that there are no known definitive sources for the number of gun shows held annually. Their estimates were based on gun shows known to the agency through the continued tracking and monitoring of known events. The number is approximate number due to the unpublicized and unregulated private sales of firearms known to members of the ATF. Although the number of gun shows known to the ATF is high, it is assumed that the number is likely much higher, as shows interested in avoiding official detection (ex. events held or attended by those interested in selling and buying stolen or illegal goods) are unlikely to advertise via conventional means. For those that are publicized, licensed vendors must complete background checks before the merchandise can be sold A similar license, however, is not required for private "collectors" who are selling to individual, private buyers from their own collections.

Table 5.3 illustrates the states holding the most gun shows each year. These data are derived from an ATF (1999) report on U.S. gun show activity. Texas was at the top of the list, hosting almost 500 events per year, and Nevada at the bottom hosting over 120. As the researcher on this project, my primary state of residence and base of operations is Ohio - which is also, conveniently, one of the states hosting the most gun shows in a typical calendar year, at a total of 148 events. So off to the gun shows I went.

Table 5.3: Primary Gun Show States

State	Number of Shows
Texas	472
Pennsylvania	250
Florida	224
Illinois	203
California	188
Indiana	180
North Carolina	170
Oregon	160
Ohio	148
Nevada	129

Adapted from a 1999 ATF report titled "Gun Shows, Brady Check and Crime Traces." Retrieved on August 8, 2007 from http://www.atf.treas.gov/pub/treas_pub/gun_show.pdf

Throughout this research adventure, I have found myself in venues ranging from large arenas that also host rock concerts and professional sporting events, to urban malls and even rural fairgrounds. The physical layout doesn't vary much, no matter whether it is a large show with 500-1000 8ft tables set up with vendor displays and 3000-5000 attendees (based on vendor and show promoter estimates) to the smallest shows attended – which still had 50 to 100 8ft vendor tables and several hundred attendees. The gun show norm is to arrange tables in a large square along the inside perimeter of the event. Within the large square are row after row of tables displaying vendor exhibits and their wares. No matter how varied the facilities, the goods, services and event set-ups (tables, displays, vendor positioning, etc.) were utterly predictable. Even the initial surprises turned out to be relatively standardized gun show features. In the end, there's not much to hide here. To quote one vendor selling shotguns at a PRO gun show that was held in the Westland Mall in Columbus, Ohio, "We've got a lot of guns!" To be sure, they (the gun dealers) have, indeed, got a lot of guns. There are, however, a variety of auxiliary services provided at gun shows that may momentarily draw your attention away from the fine buffet of cold blue steel. Notwithstanding, the services always seem to be somehow connected to guns or related items, and serve to further color and augment the breadth of the gun world. The final, overall effect of the myriad displays inside of gun shows, even the smaller shows, is comparable to a street fair or carnival midway atmosphere. There is a lot to see, and it takes some considerable effort and time to sort it all out and begin to make sense of it.

Gun events encompass a sea of human emotion. To step into the world of the gun, one must be prepared for a lesson in symbolic value, historical meaning and rich interaction rituals. A gun isn't always a gun. Sometimes a gun is an antique, a cultural artifact, an aesthetically pleasing sculpture, the memory of loved ones living and deceased, the embodiment of familial pride, and even a god-of-sorts. The following section entails what I encountered at the events listed below:

RESEARCH SCHEDULE OF EVENTS ATTENDED

1. Sharonville Civic Center I75 Exit 15 Sharonville, OH, 12/17/2005
2. Westland Mall Gun Show, Columbus, OH, 10/22/06
3. Roberts Centre, Wilmington, OH, 10/28/2006
4. Veterans Day Gun Show, University Mall, Athens, OH, 11/11/06
5. OU Second Amendment Club "Shoot Your Textbook Day, Athens, OH 11/15/06
6. Scioto Territory Desperados Shooting Tournament, Chillicothe, OH 11/19/2006
7. 7.The Oil Palace, Tyler, TX, 1/1/2007
8. Scioto Territory Desperados Shooting Tournament, Chillicothe, OH, 4/15/2007

9. 9.Hara Arena 1001 Shiloh Springs Rd Dayton, OH,6/16/2007
10. 10.Hara Arena 1001 Shiloh Springs Rd Dayton,OH, 6/17/2007
11. Fairgrounds 735 Lafayette Medina, OH, 6/23/2007
12. Roberts Centre I71 Exit 50 Wilmington, OH, 6/30/07
13. Cuyahoga Cty Fairgrounds Bagle RD Berea, OH, 7/7/07
14. Scioto Territory Desperados Shooting Tournament, Chillicothe, OH 8/19/2007
15. 15 Summit Cty Fairgrnds Arena Rt 91 & Howe Rd Akron, OH, 9/22/07
16. 16 Eastwood Mall Expo Center Rt 422 West Of Rt 46 Niles, OH, 9/29/07
17. 17.Sharonville Civic Center I75 Exit 15 Sharonville, OH, 10/13/07
18. 18 Scioto Territory Desperados Shooting Tournament, Chillicothe, OH 10/21/2007
19. Cuyahoga Cty Fairgrounds, Berea, OH, 10/27/2007
20. Summit Cty Fairgrnds Arena, Akron, OH, 11/3/2007
21. Eastwood Mall Expo Center, Niles, OH, 12/1/2007

WHAT TO EXPECT TO FIND AT YOUR LOCAL GUN SHOW?

When attending a gun show, the first indication that you have entered into a new world, with its own symbolism, is what you find in the parking lot. The first thing that caught my eye while pulling up to my first gun event were three very distinctive automobiles parked in close proximity to my car. Two of them, a Mercedes C300 luxury sedan and a BMW 328 convertible, I thought, were very out of place at a gun show. The third vehicle, a Ford F-450 "Super Duty" pick-up truck, was a closer approximation to what I had envisioned. At each event attended, there were, to be sure, plenty of big trucks; however, there were also always new Cadillacs, BMWs, and Mercedes in the mix. What the Mercedes, BMW and Ford F-450 that I parked close to at my first gun show had in common, however, were gun-related bumper stickers prominently displayed on the rear of the vehicle. Without ever meeting them, and prior to ever stepping into the formal entrance of the event, the owners of guns were already communicating something to the outside world through the messages on their varied automobiles.

Each owner had his or her own story – a story emphasized or augmented via a fairly inexpensive form of visual media. As I did not actually match the automobile owners up with their respective bumper sticker, the sticker message is listed below by automobile make. Although I recognize that it is impossible to imbue intent and meaning onto a vehicle driver/owner based on no more than a bumper sticker's text, what is relevant here is the strong, direct imagery setting the stage as a prelude to the world about to unfold before me. These messages were not quite as ominous as a caveat emptor, or Dante's famous "abandon hope all ye who enter," but very direct and powerful:

BMW Sticker: "An Armed Society is a Polite Society."

Mercedes Sticker: "Ted Kennedy's Car has Killed More People Than my Gun."

Ford F-450 Super Duty: "Politicians Love Unarmed Peasants."

These slogans were typical of ideologies expressed throughout this data collecting experience. Another commonality of each event that I attended was that there were enough gun-related data on the periphery of the events to make a definitive statement to all who enter. The statement is that the event about to unfold is highly emotional, and one that espouses an odd marriage of *inclusion* and *paranoia*. By inclusion, I am referring to the fact that each event is bulging with a variety of both overt and subtle welcome signs to recruit participants. By paranoia, I am referring to the signage and literature directly stating who or what is not welcome, and what participants should fear.

Paranoia

My first exposure to the exclusion and paranoia prevalent at gun events was a sign displayed outside of the main entrance of a PRO gun show in a Columbus Ohio Mall. The sign read "NO GANG COLORS PARAPHANALIA OR BANDANNAS ALLOWED INSIDE THE GUN SHOW." Interestingly, prior to entering the event, I observed a young man walking around inside the gun show who was dressed in a civil war confederate soldier's uniform, just on the other side of the storefront window. He was walking around a knife display directly behind the anti-gang sign. My initial impression was that as a citizen, I think that I would prefer seeing guns and knives sold to patrons wearing bandanas than confederate soldier uniforms. There's just something disquieting about the idea of arming those aligning themselves with soldiers who actively fought to uphold slavery. At least in this case, however, my initial impression was a little off center. I spoke with the attendee long enough to discern that he was not, in fact, a confederate soldier sympathizer. In fact, if anything, he was overtly insistent that his purpose was exactly the opposite. He was a history teacher who had been actively involved with two separate Ohio-based, civil war reenactment groups, the Ohio 49th Volunteer Infantry, Company H of Tiffin, Ohio, and the 4th Ohio Volunteer Federal Infantry Regiment, Company B of Lima, Ohio. He commented that he wore the confederate uniform as a reminder of "mistakes that we, as a nation, have made as a group." I later found civil war enthusiasts and re-enactors to be a common feature at gun events. At least one patron in a civil war uniform was present at most of the shows I attended.

Some of the paranoia manifest at gun shows is clearly warranted. Lest any of the attendees forget that they are surrounded by functional weapons and assorted instruments of death, a series of warning signs to patrons and vendors alike were widely posted and circulated both inside and outside of gun events (including event-related websites).

Vendor Rules

Where the vendors are concerned, a series of rules and regulations were posted that protected them, the show promoters and the customers, as well. Although not all of the rules were observed, typical rules for dealers included issues such as: dealers must sign an agreement promising to observe all Federal, State and Local laws pertaining to the sale and transfer of firearms; no loaded guns or ammunition clips allowed inside the physical facilities; dealers must ensure that guns are unloaded prior to handing them to a customer; many shows require that, prior to the purchase and transfer of guns that they remain secured by security devices (such as alarm-activated cables) inside of glass containers; vendor holster displays are not to be displayed with real/working guns – fake or plastic guns are allowed; weapons requiring black powder may be displayed and sold, but explosive black powder is not allowed inside of the physical facilities; all live ammunition is either to be sealed in its original containers or stored in something like a zip-lock bag; vendors selling portable self-defense containers such as mace or pepper-spray must ensure that it is never discharged by keeping them in their factory-sealed packaging; and tasers (portable, hand-held devices designed to incapacitate an assailant via a mild, non-lethal electric current) are only allowed to be powered-up during pre-scheduled and approved demonstrations (but never when presented to attendees).

Similarly, gun show promoters post signs warning that rule violations are immediate grounds for vendor removal from the premises (with no refund). As a frequent attendee, I was very surprised to find that show promoters continually insisted that all items put on display "must be Gun & Knife show related" (ex. guns, knife, military supplies, hunting and fishing items). Promoters warn than items not conforming to this format are subject to removal unless prior consent is granted by promoter. However, as will be illustrated later in this chapter, vendors do sell a variety of items that have no direct correlation with guns, knives, the military, hunting or fishing, such as bumper stickers, all-purpose t-shirts and hats.

Patron Safety

It is clear that in addition to liability concerns for the show promoters, public/attendee safety is at the heart of the vendor rules delineated. There are, however, also rules that are posted more specifically for attendees. In the state of Ohio, where I attended all but one event, and also in Texas, where I attended one event for both comparison and to work toward demonstrating theoretical saturation, attendees were allowed to bring their own guns to the shows to try and trade or sale. In fact, although it is discouraged by show promoters, independent "collectors" and private owners of guns frequently show up early and try to sell guns or make trades right in the parking lot. This practice, however, is not tolerated from vendors, registered or not. Due to the fact that so many guns are literally walking around, some of the following attendee safety rules are commonly displayed at gun events: make sure that guns remained unloaded at all times; double check all ammunition clips/magazines and weapon chambers to ensure they are empty before entering the show; check your weapons with attendees at the registration area or entrance; ALWAYS keeps weapons pointed safely (up or down), and never at other show-goers; keep gun chambers empty and open or plugged with safety flags/stops so attendants can verify that the gun is empty; .vendors and patrons who bring loaded clips/magazines or weapons (intentionally or not) into a gun event will be denied admission (and some signs read that violators may be subject to prosecution, as well); and NEVER attempt to load a weapon on the premises. Other frequent attendee warnings state that anyone unfamiliar with a gun's operation should leave all handling to trained personnel. Also, for attendees residing in the state of Ohio, signs constantly assert that you must be 21 or older to purchase, sell or handle a handgun and 18 or older to purchase, sell or handle a rifle or shotgun. Finally, although I continually observed children unaccompanied by adults at gun events, posted signs at each event attended specify that all attendees under the age of 18 must be accompanied by a legal guardian aged 21 or older.

Inclusion

Who are welcome? Judging only by the most frequent signs that I encountered, the following are welcome:

- The police
- The military
- Firefighters
- Families with children
- Registered Vendors
- Women?
- Racial Minorities?
- Liberal Democrats?

At all of the gun shows I have attended, the *police, firefighters, military* personnel on active duty and *veterans* of foreign wars were admitted either free or at a reduced rate. Similarly, *children and women* are typically admitted free of charge. However, children rarely accounted for more than about 5% of those in attendance. Women appear to be of interest to the promoters of gun shows. There is no shortage of literature and items tailor made for women at these events;

and, women do make up approximately 15% of those in attendance, including staff/personnel, (based on observations and vendor accounts). Most shows have at least two vendor tables set up with designer guns marketed toward women and children, such as the pink or polka dotted .22 caliber "Cricket" rifles. For the modern woman who prefers to pack a pistol, Ohio's Conceal and Carry Laws just might necessitate a designer "Conceal and Carry Handbag." Or as one of the vendor signs read, "Get Your Conceal & Carry Handbags Here." To the left of the table was the typical shotgun broker, and to the immediate right was another vendor selling cookbooks and aprons. One of their signs read, "For those who like to kill it and grill it."

Many of the exchanges and attitudes that I encountered while making observations at gun events were counter to the words of welcome on the physical signage. As my accounts will reveal in some detail, more often than not, women were the subject of ridicule and relegated to a second-class status in the gun world, at best. Gun *vendors* are happy to take their money, but would clearly rather deal with men, who they feel will be more likely to result in a sale. I continually encountered attitudes similar to those expressed by a high end pistol vendor at a Cincinnati, Ohio area, show who commented after a woman stopped by to ask questions about a Colt handgun

> …I knew she wasn't going to buy anything. That girl wasted by time and probably cost me at least two potential customers.

Multiple vendors also expressed that although these shows are really "for the men," when they see a couple attending together, they feel that they are more likely to close a deal. As a Columbus, Ohio, vendor shared

> …if he drags her in with him, she is probably looking to buy him a gift…and wants him to pick it out, or he is picking something out for her to learn to shoot or protect herself when he's not around…

Even observing interaction surrounding new "designer" guns that are marketed expressly for women and children, I observed that the attitudes expressed by the vendors were very different when pitching their prods for men or women. When women were present,

The vendors had a tendency to make comments like "you need this cute, little gun," "isn't this pretty," or "this might match your purse," It is important to note that during the entire course of this research project, the word "cute" was not used even once in the verbal exchanges between two men to discuss the properties of their guns. Additionally, vendors trying to pitch the same designer guns to men have a very different approach. They will often apologize for the gun being pink. One Roberts Center, Ohio vendor had a whole story line developed to diffuse the less-than-masculine color or the pink and polka dotted "cricket" rifles by appealing to the utilitarian practicality of a pink gun in cold-weather climates. As he explained

Vendor: Maybe if she has one of these, you'll get a chance to shoot more too.

Patron: I don't know if I really want a pink gun sitting in my gun rack.

Vendor: I've heard that some hunters up in Alaska actually prefer these pink guns now for hunting. Hunters are always losing their guns in the snow. Pink really stands out, so she'll be less likely to lose it.

Symbolic Usurpation

Although I noted the same phenomenon occurring regularly in the context of a gun show environment, it was at the live action cowboy tournaments and other shooting events where I was overwhelmed by the relative ease with which males symbolically empower themselves by usurping the hegemonic masculine capital of the gun. The transactions involving gun-related symbolic capital were seamless, with the final product of the empowered male appearing as natural as breathing. For females, the exchanges were far more awkward, even appearing graceless and forced. The posted signs say "women welcome," but the often not-so-subtle signs of another type declare in a loud and decisive voice that this is definitely not their world. This section further explores symbolic empowerment within a gun event framework, providing an overview of relevant literature and real-world examples of this highly complex, multi-faceted process in motion.

I made all observations of live action cowboy role players at an old-west style target range called "Desperadoville." Desperadoville, home of a cowboy shooting club called the "Scioto Territory Desperados" is located on the outskirts of Chillicothe, Ohio. It is tucked away into the hills in an area likely only stumbled upon by those who are truly lost and those who have come to shoot. While driving down a dusty, gravel road to reach the complex, it is not difficult to imagine how the architects of the facility found their creative inspiration. It is a mock old western town, with a saloon that is used for lunch and meetings, and a series of stages (shooting areas) that resemble barns, old banks, country stores, etc (see images 5.1 through 5.4 below). "The goal was to make it as fun and authentic as possible for a bunch of us who love to play cowboy or are cowboys at heart," says Osa Hunter, secretary of the Desperados organization.

Image 5.1: Desperadoville Enactment Area

Image 5.2: Desperadoville Tournament Staging Area 1

Image 5.3: Desperadoville Staging Area 2

Image 5.4: Desperadoville Staging Area 3

Image 5.5: Scioto Territory Desperados Tournament in Progress 1

Image 5.6: Scioto Territory Desperados Tournament in Progress 2

Most gender-related research has narrowly focused on the different rates of participation for men and women in specific activities and behaviors (Connell 1987; West 1987). This approach to studying and understanding gender has ignored everything that exists beyond the boundaries of the reproductive arena (Connell 2001). Since the 1970's, however, many researchers have suggested that gender is not a mere biological distinction. Gender appears to be achieved via a far more complex social process involving culture, structure and interaction (Connell 1987; Martin and Jurik 1996; Messner 2002; West 1987). U.S. gun culture is a fruitful vantage point from which to analyze the complex process of gender construction and enactment that has gone, until now, relatively unexplored by the academic community.

Although many researchers have stressed the importance of structural characteristics and resource access in gender construction (Courtenay 2000 and Messerschmidt 2000), most work has focused on the direct effects of biological sex on various outcomes, accepting structural influences as a pre-existing (but largely untested) condition. This approach takes a peek inside of the structures that condition gender, treating gender as a type of "structured action" similar to race and social class that we produce and reproduce contextually, depending on the setting and gender capital available in a given situation (Connell 1987; Messerschmidt 1997; West and Zimmerman 1987).

Building on West and Zimmerman's (1987) concept of "doing gender," Messerschmidt's (1997) theory of gender as structured action, the notion of gender fluidity or a gender continuum is illustrated by Connell's (1987, 1995) concept of hegemonic masculinity and emphasized femininity. Here, Connell identifies typified, dominant forms of gender that are not determined by biological sex, but are socially reinforced, glorified and constructed in relation to "oppositional masculinities and femininities" (Messerschmidt 1997: 9-10). Not only does this process of doing oppositional gender difference reinforce the erroneous notion of gender distinction by sex (the reproductive arena), it also emphasizes a preference for gender conformity that more closely approximates the typified/appropriate male and female behavior, and facilitates the formation of a sexualized hierarchy and various forms of gender stratification (Martin and Jurik 1996; Olsen 1990).

GUNS: A MASCULINE SYMBOL OF POWER

Although Durkheim (1965/1912) focused on rituals central to religious practices and not gun culture, his approach to rituals is highly applicable to this study. According to Durkheim, rituals speak to our identity as a common people. They do more than provide a cohesive rallying point to help ensure social cohesion: rituals help us define who we are and how we got here. By approaching any ritual with this understanding, rituals can provide us with valuable insight about the core values, beliefs and prevalent social structures associated with the group practicing a ritual.

Equally valuable, however, are notably absent rituals. In this case, that of the female gun owner and user, there are well-defined rituals related to *male* gun heroes. However, the practices of being a gun person and receiving appropriate gun user feedback appear to assume that the hero wielding the socially constructed instrument of power will be male. According to Amy Cox (2007), the acceptance of guns as an extension of masculinity is directly related to early U.S. history. Cox points out that guns in early America were a practical tool used by men to hunt, defend himself from wild Animals and Native Americans – and protect his family. There was also a connection of guns and bravery, along the same lines as the famous Revolutionary War uttering: "Don't shoot until you see the whites of their eyes." Through the course of time the gun has shifted from being a tool of survival into a symbol for masculinity.

Many gun owners today consider ownership as a large part of our nation's history, but Cox demonstrated shifts in the symbolic meaning of guns in the U.S. over time. Both subtle and extreme shifts have occurred in areas concerning the protection of family and country. With the outbreak of the revolutionary war guns started being interchanged with words such as freedom and liberty. This made the gun more symbolic because it stood for something else rather than just a utilitarian survival aid. It was also the men who went out and fought the war with these guns. Another idea presented by Cox is the idea of what defined masculinity during this early time period. In colonial times, men were supposed to marry, have families, run a strict household, and protect their families (142). They would constantly use their guns to protect not necessarily shooting trespassers but by keeping wild animals away from livestock and crops.

It is not until the turbulent 20th century, with increased media attention and heightened public awareness of violent gun use (ex. prohibition-era mob violence, violent protests and assassinations surrounding civil rights, gun-related death sensitivity surrounding the Vietnam war, and the media saturation of drug war-related violence of the 1980s) that we see the legitimate, "normal" masculine symbolic value of guns being notably challenged (Cox 2007; Cramer 1999; Korwin 1995). As a direct result, there appears to be no comparable ritual practice of traditional symbolic empowerment for females who venture into the male gun arena or their social audience. Females are indeed "welcome," at least on the surface. However, unlike the male, who may recognize the symbolic masculine power ascribed to a gun and usurp it as part of his masculine performance, the female gun owner and operator is not similarly situated. "In real life, women who use guns in a violent way are ostracized. Guns are perhaps the best cultural example of how the imaginary and the real cannot be conflated:

there is a fatal world of difference between props in fantasies and real guns that have the power to kill" (Browder 2006: 232).

MEDIA IMAGES AS AN INSTITUTIONAL INFLUENCE

As was illustrated in the section on popular culture and popular music, media images pertaining to men, women and guns depict two distinct sets of gun images, expectations and behaviors for men and women. I demonstrated that a variety of layouts and song lyrics characterized males purchasing and wielding guns for the sheer joy of it as well as the "bad ass" empowerment or charge associated with the gun. Females, however, were either depicted exclusively as sport shooters (on rare occasions), and as would-be-victims. When they were empowered by the presence of the gun, it was either as a source of protection, in retaliation for being victimized, or as the student of a man who was teaching her the right way to use a gun.

What is the impact of these separate images of men, women and guns? In Goffman's (1979) *Gender Advertisements*, he explores the arrangement and use of male and female images in 20th century advertising. His work significantly contributes to our understanding of the way images may be used to communicate social information. More importantly, for the purpose of studying gender dynamics, Goffman also illuminates the manner in which media images have been incorporated into our social expectations. He described gender advertisements as "both shadow and substance: they show what we wish or pretend to be" (15). This becomes relevant in that we use these images to assign gender value to objects and concepts.

A certain level of gender capital can be ascribed to a product, idea or event, depending on the way that it is packaged and marketed. Majors and Billson (1992) found this to be true of several activities that were successfully entrenched in a hegemonic masculine identity via effective media image saturation. These activities included "smoking, drug and alcohol abuse, fighting, sexual conquests, dominance and crime" (34). These activities and rituals, according to Courtenay (2000) and Majors and Billison (1992) can be viewed as a side effect of the compulsion to achieve hegemonic masculinity. Lacking other gender resources, these activities become a form of "symbolic empowerment," or a ready-made source of masculine capital.

Jiobu and Curry (2001) discuss the symbolic empowerment associated with gun ownership. Although Messerschmidt, Courtenay and Majors and Billison do not use the term "symbolic empowerment," they appear to be addressing the same concept. Masculine resources are in some way threatened or challenged, gun use or ownership and various high risk behaviors become recognizable sources of instant masculine capital.

According to Messerschmidt (1990), the formation and enactment of masculinity or any other form of gender is contingent on available "masculine resources." Messerschmidt (2000) and Courtenay (2000) also address the notion of "masculinity challenges," and how structural barriers to achieving hegemonic masculinity can have negative consequences that result in some men and women developing negativistic strategies for claiming gender resources. This also suggests something very positive, however. If gender is something that we actively work to accomplish, gender responses can be altered by recognizing and modifying contributing structures, rituals, and our subsequent actions. In "High Noon," Gary Cooper's character didn't have to be brave, and it was clear that he didn't want to be there in the streets at noon. When he put the gun in his hand, he empowered himself. There was no longer a trace of fear in his countenance. His fear presented a "masculinity challenge," he was able to "symbolically empower" himself with the gun, and his audience was ultimately satisfied with his appropriate, masculine, gendered performance.

PROTECTING THE MASCULINE CENTER OF GUNS

Connell (2000) discussed various "toxic consequences" of the ongoing effort of males to achieve some idealized form of masculinity. These consequences range from acts of violence various risk behaviors and unhealthy practices. The underlying commonality appears to be the link between these toxic consequences and the structured performance of gender. As Messerschmidt (1997 and 2000) discusses, as males face masculinity challenges in the pursuit of hegemonic masculinity, they will take advantage of gender resources that are contextually available. Through the process of symbolic empowerment, both the concept of gun ownership and the physical object, the gun itself, have been ascribed a certain level of masculine capital that are available to be claimed – by men. Messner (2002) writes about the masculine center of sports, and the difficulty of females to negotiate the center. This notion of the masculine center is highly applicable to gun culture. Men will actively protect the masculine center of sport (Messner 2002). The vignettes below demonstrate the validity of the proactively protected masculine center of guns and guns use, the toxic consequences of doing masculinity and the difficulties women face while negotiating the masculine center of gun culture. These conversation fragments took place during a shooting tournament at the Scioto Territory Desperados "Desperadoville" complex, as a female and male informant tried to fill me in on the wide-range of participants at the site:

> Female Informant – "They let several women shoot here, and did you see our girl? Oh she's just so cute. She's only ten. You've got to see her shoot that big double-barrel. She's not scared at all."

> Male Informant – "Have you seen the Kid? He's great! Only 14, and the boy's a natural. That kind of skill is rare. He can empty a gun faster than I can squeeze off two rounds."

There are a few recurring themes illustrated by these two examples. In terms of the center of guns being masculine and protected, here we have another example of women finding it difficult to simply empower themselves by taking up arms. Focusing on the language, we can see that the female informant who is wanting me to know that women are treated as equals at least at this particular venue didn't catch that she was telling me that "they" (the men) "let" the women and girls shoot there – implying than men are still in the dominant position and women must have their permission to be there – or anywhere. This social arrangement was commented on by Browder (2006), who eloquently observed that "guns remain a charged symbol of women's access to full citizenship" (230). Rampant examples in gun culture like the one provided above underscore the significance of Browder's contention, and just how highly contested this barrier to full citizenship remains. Also, similar to what was noted in popular gun literature and song analyses, when the girl is the subject matter, she is reduced to being "cute," and it's a big deal just that she isn't terrified of the gun. In the case of the boy, he's "a natural," he's got rare "skill," and he's "the kid," a very cool cowboy, respectful moniker. Another patron referred to him as "Cool Hand Luke," which is another reference to media, and a bold and gutsy character portrayed by Paul Newman in a 1960s movie of the same name.

DEFERENCE AND DEMEANOR-BASED GUN RITUALS

In the course of collecting gun stories and the meaning of guns from gun collectors, a series of ritual themes emerged through both the active telling of their stories and observations of ritual activities surrounding the use and ownership of guns. This section provides a candid look at these rituals and their function in gun culture. The standard for studying rituals in the social sciences was established by Emile Durkheim with his (1965/1912) *Elementary Forms of the Religious Life*. Durkheim depicted rituals as both "determined modes of action" (51) and "rules of conduct which prescribe how a man should comport himself in the presence of sacred objects" (56).

Building on Durkheim, Spencer and Comte's social evolutionary models of human development, Turner (2000) and Goffman (1967), asserted that at our current state of social evolution, it is impossible for human social interaction to exist without the assistance of "interaction rituals." Rituals, which are typically "emotion-arousing," are used to begin and end all interactions, and also set the stage for everything that occurs socially in between (Turner 2000). Goffman (1967) expanded on Durkheim's sacred-centric definition of rituals, adding that rituals "represent ways in which the individual must guard and design the symbolic implications of his acts while in the immediate presence of an object that has a special value for him" (57).

Birrell (1981) argued that Goffman's broader definition promises greater application value of rituals as a site of social observations, in that it is not limited to rare subject matter that is set aside as sacred. Guns present an interesting vantage point from which to observe rituals, in that they lend support to both Durkheim and Goffman's approach to studying rituals. In true Durkheimian fashion, some of the gun owners clearly depict their guns as sacred objects that are "awe inspiring," and something to be set aside and revered. Others gun owners, however, lean far more toward Goffman's point of view, describing their guns as important, meaningful and "special," but by no means on the same level as an authentic object of religious worship. Whether depicted as "sacred" or simply "special and meaningful," the world of the gun is rich with ritual activity surrounding their use. Goffman (1967) argued that ritual activity contains certain basic components (56). Two such ritual components that Goffman identified are "deference" and demeanor."

Deference is characterized by Goffman (1967) as "the appreciation an individual shows of another to that other, whether through avoidance rituals or presentational rituals (77). Much deferential behavior comes in the form of something paid by subordinates to those in charge (59). There are cases, however, when those in positions of relative authority also owe deferential treatment to their subordinates; such as: a boss giving annual reviews and raises for a job well done; everyone, regardless of rank, honoring the dead or offering compassion to the terminally ill, etc (59). Finally, deference may also be extended to someone perceived as an equal or even subservient, when praising them for some perceived skill or talent (59).

Ritual *demeanor* is what Goffman refers to as (that element of the individual's ceremonial behavior typically conveyed through deportment, dress, and bearing, which serves to express to those in his immediate presence that he is a person of certain desirable or undesirable qualities (77). These qualities are ultimately conveyed to announce to other recipients engaged in the ritual how to respond to the "demeaned individual." More specifically, Goffman observed that these two separate components of ritual behavior "represent ways in which an actor celebrates and confirms his relation to a recipient" (1967: 56-57).

Although Goffman focused his attention exclusively on individuals as recipients of such celebratory treatment and respect, he concedes, however, that the social and recipient are not necessarily both individuals. There are some well-documented instances of individual social actors offering up respectful treatment to objects, such as crucifixes and altars, and even non-spiritual objects, such as saluting a flag – and in the case of this research project, guns (57).

In this section, I identify specific rituals observed among my gun informants. Although deference and demeanor are complementary, and not mutually exclusive in ritual activity, without exception, these two components are present and operating as part of the gun-related rituals discussed herein.

Celebrating the Gun

One series of ritual themes manifest in these data actively seek to celebrate a gun or guns in different way. Most notably are rituals surrounding the *presenting, talking up, retiring* and *naming* of guns.

Presenting Ritual

Whether it is in the homes of gun collectors, a gun show exhibit hall or a shooting event, rituals involving the presentation of guns are undeniable. Some forms of presentation are more overt, such as the tendency of guns to be displayed in cabinets or case displays based on their relative value or importance to the owner or seller. The colt single action army 1873 model (see image 6.7) featured on display at an Ohio Gun, Knife and Military show is typical of guns of this type displayed for sale at gun shows. The glass case (and typically an armed alarm cable) may seem a reasonable presentation showcase for a gun that can command up to $60,000 in excellent condition, and even $10,000 in poor condition (Sildeler, 2008).

Image 5.7: Colt single action army 1873 model

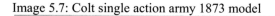

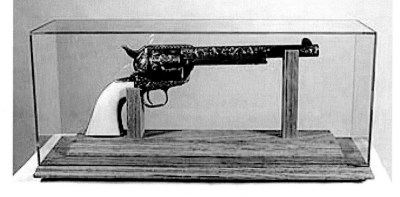

Images 5.8 and 5.9 highlight an even more extreme mode of presentation in the form of the rare but available, rotating pedestal/lighted and pressurized multi-gun cabinet. These cabinets sell

for as much as $15,000, and feature the displayed guns as nothing less than a genuine object of awe, majesty and worship. The deference shown these guns is manifest: quite literally, they are something to be placed on a pedestal and admired.

Image 5.8: Rotating pedestal/lighted and pressurized multi-gun cabinet

Image 5.9: Rotating pedestal/lighted and pressurized multi-gun cabinet

More than one conference attendee and several show attendees freely offered-up that the rotating cabinets (see Image 5.9) are fairly rare, they are also reserved for the best of the best, and sometimes as a reminder to keep the hands off the valued goods. Perhaps more revealing is what various informants explained to be about position. It is often the case among gun owners that the position of the gun within the cabinet also says something about its significance. The most prized will occupy a specific place of honor. Also, as my informant with the largest collection of guns stressed, "the fact that a gun is even in one of my cases of gun safes means something. I've got hundreds that are just crated. The ones that are out are intended to be seen."

There are, however also presentations related to guns that don't involve their physical housing or display. Just in the simple act of a gun owner handing a gun to someone else to view, a deference and demeanor-guided ritual takes place. At gun shows, for instance, the vendors don't just hand guns over to would-be clientele. They make a show of formally presenting the gun as something highly valued, desirable, and precious to hold. Great care is taken in the handing over of the gun. It is never just shoved into someone's hand. Guns are exchanged with a great deal of reverence, as if something delicate, and not a piece of metal and wood is being handled. The demeanor of the vendor indicates that this is something to be taken seriously, and that they are to be taken equally seriously. The presenting of the gun and handing off of the gun is typically immediately preceded or followed-up with a comment like "isn't she a beauty," "check out the weight on that baby," "note the fine attention to detail and exquisite craftsmanship," "our ancestors sure took pride in their work," etc. The deference to both the guns and the audience is also well defined. The gun is precious and to be treated as nothing less. The audience, depending on how they present themselves, with either the demeanor of an amateur or expert, receives the deference appropriate for a student/trainee, or accomplished and skilled expert, respectively.

In the homes of collectors, I noticed similar types of interactions. As guns were being passed from the hand of the owner to my own, whether is was a $200 single action Ruger .357 single action revolver, or rare Colt Dragoon worth thousands, they were handed over in a presentational manner, typically with both hands under the gun, and always with a look of pride and reverence. This set the stage for me, the audience, in signaling that I was in receipt of something to be respected. I was also being informed, depending on the history of the gun, that I was submissive either to the presenter for their expertise (or out of appreciation of the desirable item they possessed), or the awe-inspiring gun because of its special qualities. The end result of deference paid to the gun or being appropriately demeaned toward the owner for his knowledge, skill or expertise is essentially the same: the owner/presenter of the gun has used the gun as part of the interaction to be in receipt of deferential treatment. It is in violation of interaction rules for him/her to defer to themselves, but they have effectively used the gun to ask for and receive it. The owner has essentially not only presented a gun possessing fine qualities to the audience, but also what he/she considers to be among their finest or desirable qualities, as well. They consider the gun and its many fine qualities to be representative of their own fine and praiseworthy qualities.

At gun shows, there is also a tendency for gun presentation to be influenced by the rank or pecking order of the vendors. These events are highly stratified, with high-end dealers typically getting prime locations along the perimeter walls, stand alone displays, and set apart from what I often heard referred to as "junk brokers," (ex. those selling random, inexpensive shotguns or pistols, books, knives, hunting supplies and clothing). I have observed that not only does the demeanor of the high-end vendors suggest that the items they have to present are superior to the "junk vendors," the "junk vendors," with their deference to the high-end vendors suggests that they are in an accord. As I heard one vendor quip to a customer: "I'm not selling art, just cheap, used guns. If you want something nice, see the antique brokers in the corner booths." I also noted, however, that this self-proclaimed "cheap, used gun" dealer, when handing over arms to a customer for inspection, handed them over with the same care as the "antique" dealers located in the corner booths.

The Scioto Territory Desperados demonstrated additional aspects of presenting as a type of celebration. Here the deference and demeanor surrounding the presenting of a gun for inspection was based on a combination of the rarity and value of the gun, and the acknowledged skill level of the cowboy marksman. The best of the best tended to have a decidedly more cocky and elitist demeanor. I still found them to be approachable, but the way in which they presented their guns for show suggested that you (the audience) was supposed to offer up a high degree of deference, and recognize the privilege being offered up. When these cowboys handed over their guns, they always offered up technical specs about the guns, such as the model, how many were manufactured, and often how much it cost, as well. One cowboy shooter told me that he had loved the Lone Ranger's pearl handled pistols as a kid and modeled his collection accordingly. I got the distinct impression when I was handling the guns that I was supposed to be as moved to hold them as I would if I were actually holding the pistols wielded by the Lone Ranger himself. I also noticed that the participants who shot using less-expensive replicas offered up a higher degree of deference to those who had vintage weapons – as if only those with authentic models could be real cowboys, worthy of deference. In fact, many of those shooting with less expensive replica models were apologetic that they did not have "fancier" guns to show me. Nonetheless, although these cowboy shooters showed one another varying levels of deference and demeanor based on skill level and ordinance type, it did not change the fact that the least-skilled shooters, and those with the least-expensive models handed over or presented their guns with a high level of care and respect for the gun – even if they were ultimately apologizing that the gun was "not fancier." In the end, even the least presentation-worthy guns received what I would consider to be a high-degree of deference from the presenters.

Talking Up the Gun

The next celebrating ritual observed among my informants and other gun culture observations was the active "talking up" of the gun. By talking up the gun, I am referring to verbal exchanges wherein the owner or representative of the gun engages the recipient in a type of bragging rite. This rite, however, is not the gun-holding or occupying individual directly bragging on his/herself (although, as discussed in the last section, they may well be bragging about their own desirable qualities "through the gun"); instead, they direct all attention to the remarkable qualities of the gun. During this ritual, guns are spoken of as if they posses human or even super-human qualities. As such, guns are spoken of in the third person – just as if discussing or addressing an individual. "You've never seen anything like her. I don't think that she's ever missed," commented one informant about his Stevens/Savage 12 gauge shotgun. Another gun owner, in commenting on a deer kill that he had made from 100 yards, "this baby is amazing. Her sights are dead as nails accurate." When asked to explain "dead as nails accurate," he replied that if something stands in front of it and I pull the trigger, then anything on the other end is dead as nails."

Another informant talked up one of his guns as if to describe it as a celebrity – or at least a true celebrity among guns to be selected (see image 5.10):

The m1941 is among the rarest US WWII guns produced. They made fewer than 20,000 compared to over 3,000,000 each of the M1 Garand and M1 Carbine. A friend I met at the shooting club called me to ask if I had ever heard of a "Johnson Army Rifle." He'd never heard of it, but someone wanted to trade him it for a shotgun worth about $600. I told him I would buy it sight-unseen for at least twice that. At the time they were selling for around $2500 if you could find one. About four months later a well known author, Bruce Canfield, published a book on them, and suddenly everyone wanted one. Overnight they began selling at auctions in the $5000 to $8000 range. I have had many offers on mine, but have no intention of parting with it. Two days after I bought it my first son was born, and if I have my way it will be his some day. It was acquired in November 2001. The significance of the gun is historical - rarity, and financial. I'll admit that I enjoy most the fact that even most serious WWII US gun collectors don't have one. When a collector sees an M1941 Johnson in your collection they think "this guy must have everything". It is the type of thing that separates a collection or a display from others.

Even stronger emphasis on bragging rights and talking up the gun are emphasized in the following account:

The Russian Nagant is in itself an interesting gun, but the so-call KGB model (see image11 below) is a particularly special and rare variation. The 1895 Nagant has a unique design for a revolver, in that the cylinder moves forward to seal against the barrel. Some have said it shot more Russians than Germans in WWII because it was issued to political officers to discourage retreat. The "KGB" version was actually developed for its predecessor the NKVD. It has a smaller grip and barrel than the standard 1895 Nagant and is rare enough that most collectors have never seen one. My father was at a local gun show just a few years ago when he saw it on the table of a fellow collector. Neither my father nor the collector knew what it was, but the collector wanted $350, about twice the value of a normal 1895 at the time. My father didn't have the money so he went home without it. When he got home he did some research and learned how rare it was. He rushed back to the show. Still not having the money, he took with him a pistol worth about $700, hoping the fellow collector would trade. The man was more than willing to trade his $350 gun for my father's $700 gun. I have since been offered $3000 for it but I wouldn't sell it for twice that. From time to time I find myself talking to a collector with a more extensive collection than my own. I can always say "...sure, but I bet you don't have one of these."Then I show them the KGB model 1895. So far, I've not come across another collector that has one. So the pistol of Stalin's heavy-handed secret police is now my secret weapon in the light-hearted battle for bragging rights.

Image 5.10: WWII US M1941 Johnson. M1941. Johnson Automatics 1941.30-06.

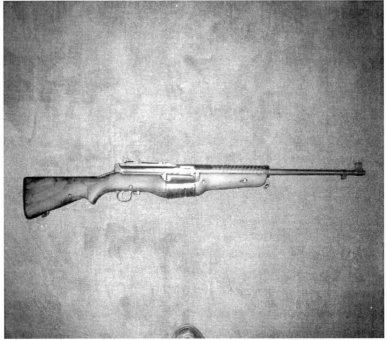

Image 5.11: Russian Nagant M1895 "KGB" Model

Although the examples discussed above were commonplace, there was another, notable component to "talking up the gun," that goes beyond the simple bragging about the gun and what it can or has done. One pattern that emerged was gun owners describing a type of cooperative relationship between them and the gun. A good kill or shot was not the simple matter of an adroit and prepared marksman with good timing. It took more than just their (the marksman's) good efforts – the gun had to perform well too. As one subject was relaying a hunting story to another attendee at a Dayton gun show about an impressive deer "harvest" made on a hunting trip in Indiana with his "prize" Thompson/Center Encore rifle, I heard him state "yeah baby, look what you did." The "you" in this story was the Thompson rifle. When I commented to the gun owner "but you're the one who made the shot," he explained to me that "every shot has limitations." He went on to explain that "it doesn't matter how good of a shot you are, you and the gun have to be working together...You have to show up, be controlled and make the shot, but that doesn't matter if the gun isn't capable of delivering results." Still another informant, a Columbus, Ohio-area highway patrolman, in discussing the guns he selected to use on patrol (a Glock model 27, and 45 back-up) observed that in addition to preferring something that was relatively comfortable as part of his uniform with decent "magazine capacity," he needed to know the "guns would be dependable, reliable, accurate and ready to perform." He went on to explain that you "really have to form a partnership with your gun in the field." User accounts like these go beyond an appreciation of guns in certain contexts, by assigning them a human-like (and sometimes super-human) quality. They are discussed as someone upon whom we rely for results...to perform...to achieve success.

Finally, though it is not technically talking, at the live action shooting events, I repeatedly observed that after a good performance, the cowboy marksmen will kiss their guns. I lumped this together with "taking up the gun," because the kiss was never delivered in silence. There is always a prelude to a kiss, or post-kiss commentary involving the active praise of the gun. Some observed pre and post-kiss comments included: "That a girl;" "Thanks old reliable;" and "You're good as gold."

Naming the Gun

Although I did not find this to be a dominant ritual among my informants, another type of gun celebrating ritual observed involves the names that some owners bestow upon their favorite guns. Naming practices appear to be reserved for guns prominent in the lives of the owners. Some are sidekick names, indicative of the cooperative relationships forged between the gun and user – as discussed in the previous section. One informant, an Ohio insurance agent, gun collector and "avid shooter," spoke fondly of a set of Ruger Colt-45 replica "New Vaquero" revolvers. He named them "Pancho and Cisco," after an early 20th century western tv series called "The Cisco Kid." He had only ever fired "Pancho," because "Pancho was the trusty sidekick." Another live action cowboy shooter had a single-action 45 that he named "Tonto," – named after the famous sidekick of the Lone Ranger.

Not all of the nicknames signaled a working relationship, however. Some of the names given to the guns celebrate some humorous aspect or some other quality or characteristic the gun was believed to posses. A Texas gun collector, a retired engineer from North Texas, for instance, had a Luger model .22 pistol in his collection that he called "the Little Nazi." This name was based exclusively on the history of the gun, as this particular model had been used widely by the German military during the Second World War.

Other gun names combined both humor and physical gun attributes. A gun collector and hunter from southeastern Ohio had a .50

caliber Hawken muzzle loaded rifle in his collection that he called
"Rowdy Yates." He picked this name for a few different reasons. One,
because the character Rowdy Yates was played by Clint Eastwood on
the 1960s television series "Rawhide." The collector not only "loved
westerns," but "Rowdy Yates was a bad mother fucker; and Clint
Eastwood, let's face it, is the coolest cowboy ever." He had settled on
the name for one other reason, however, and that being that "the gun
was so damn loud, the name Rowdy just seemed to fit."

Finally, a gun broker at a show in Berea, Ohio had a 1780s and
1820s model Blunderbuss muzzle/loaded flintlock that he had named
Bea Arthur and Hillary Rodham Clinton, respectively. "I named the
one Bea Arthur because she's just a little bigger and more intimidating
than most of her type and she's old and ugly…I call the other one
Hillary Rodham Clinton because this model shoots from the hip, but
she's also a loud bitch that shoots her mouth off."

Retiring the Gun

The ultimate celebrating of guns is displayed as part of a formal retiring
of guns. Only guns that occupy the most special and honored positions
among not only guns but also other aspects of a gun owner's life are
subject to a retirement. Gun retirements take a few different forms,
ranging from being set aside to be passed down to children or
grandchildren or made into a trophy/shrine to the gun. Retirements
also occur for reasons as varied as retirement for "exceptional service,"
to considerations of "extreme old age and deterioration." The most
common reason that I found for guns being retired was that they had
become special to the owner due to the gun's history. Sometimes it had
been passed down for multiple generations, and often, valued not only
for sentimental reasons of ancestral pride, but also because of its
history of great service within the family. As one Columbus Ohio gun
collector explained to me, "you want to retire your special guns while
they still perform well…After a big or special kill or good tournament
showing is best." As is observed in image 5.12, some gun owners
actually manage to capture part of the special moment that warranted
the retiring of a gun, by incorporating the desirable qualities or
"capabilities" of the gun into its final resting place (case, gun rack or
integrated rack/trophy).

Image 5.12: Retired 30-30 Caliber Deer Rifle Integrated Into Last Trophy Kill

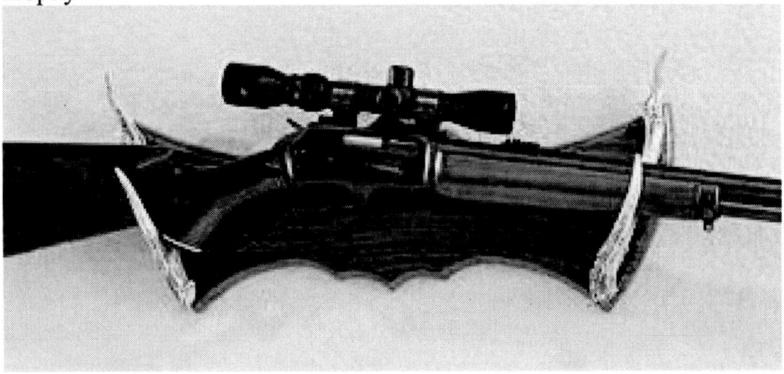

However, the retiring of a gun is often considered to be temporary, as the preparation for the presentment of the retired arm to the next generation. It is essentially the retirement of the gun for one generation only. They step down and endeavor to preserve the gun while it is still in good form and still possessing worthwhile "capabilities." At the same time, some of the value and memories tied up in the gun are perceived as far too precious to risk damaging, diminishing or losing before it can be shared with the next in line to be in receipt of the gun. This sentiment was expressed by a variety of gun owners who had "retired" a gun from their own personal use, but eagerly awaited the appropriate time to pass them along to their sons, daughters or grandchildren.

"Time Capsuling" and "Refreshing Recollections"

According to Connell (1987 and 2000), our gender performances are, at least in part, tied to our emotional attachments or cathexis. On a general level, cathexis is the active clinging to or embracing of ideas and objects on a deeply meaningful level. In the time honored traditions of typical Judeo-Christian wedding vows, the notion of "to have and to hold" exemplifies the deep, "cathetic" embracing of something. Ritual activity involving guns as emotional cathexis was readily apparent among my informants. However, with guns, the owners go through something more than basic cathexis. Some are using the guns to preserve memories and history, which I have to think of as "time capsuling," whereas others use them to travel back in time and relive or refresh experiences lived long ago – actively recreating events and people, the way they were, in their minds. The latter process is referred to here as "refreshing recollections." Each will be explored through the examples provided by participants. According to Collins (2004), "the emotional intensity that symbols had while fresh begins to cool, their life dependant, like all symbols, on the intensity of the gatherings in which they will again be invoked" (95).

In order to have and to hold the symbolic power imbued in a gun, there first must exist a unique level of deference to the gun, as well as an acknowledgement of the symbolic power or significance of the gun. Most of the clinging fast to guns that I noticed centered on memories tied to specific guns, the longing for times past, values associated with gun use – such as the right to bear arms – and other values and traditions related to guns and their history. In sharing stories about his three favorite guns, one of my collectors addressed various aspects of cathexis, including deference to the gun's performance, shared experiences with the gun and the importance of deep family memories tied directly to the guns (see image 5.13 for a photo of the guns in the order discussed below).

> My Hawken 50 Caliber Muzzleloader was built by my father. It is as fine a gun that you could ever want. Dad took it hunting once after he built it and missed a deer in the pouring rain because of a misfire. He decided that he was done hunting after that. I eventually bought the gun from him. I fired it twice and it was as accurate as it was good looking. I remember watching dad build the gun, how his hands looked as he fit, polished and blued the metal, how he meticulously fit the wood and the metal together, and the attention that he paid to detail in the final finishing of the gun. This gun reminds me of my dad. It is an example of the care that he took to do things as good as they could be done. He is still alive but his memories are escaping from him now and he can no longer fix things or build fine guns.
>
> I used my Marlin Model 25, 22 Magnum rifle a lot at a time when I had very little money. I had just moved back to South

East Ohio from California and had not yet started a job. Luckily it was in the autumn of the year. I had maintained my membership in a local shooting club and had 40 plus acres where I could hunt and fish. In addition I had access to family owned land. I used that little rifle to take as many squirrel as I could eat, as many rabbits as I saw, and would have used it for deer had it been legal to do so. It kept me in meat for as long as the season lasted and I had started a job. It is not a fancy gun, just a bolt action; clip fed 22 magnum rifle which has a low power scope. Whenever I pick up this gun, I know that I can depend upon it.

The 50 Caliber H & R Sidekick Muzzleloader was the first "modern" muzzleloader that I owned. It was a discount clearance buy from a sporting goods catalog. Whenever I pick it up, brings back the memories of several years in deer camp with my brother and friends. That gun never let me down. I think that I took every deer that I shot at with that gun. The last time that I used it was a cold, quiet day with heavy snow coming down. I sat on my favorite deer stand, just enjoying the quiet and the beauty of the woods. Memories of the hunts, and the time spent with good company are there any time I handle that gun.

In the details about the first gun, the owner's accounts of the memory of his father working with the gun, the way his father's hands looked when handling the gun, and the importance of preserving memories of a time when his father was healthier and more youthful come through strongly. The account of why he valued the second gun, a rifle that was "not fancy" or valuable in terms of monetary worth, we can see a little overlap of celebrating the gun and a partnership forged with the gun. It is clear the owner felt indebted to the gun for helping to keep him fed when times were hard and he literally struggled to keep meat on the table. With the third gun, the owner states that he can't pick up the gun without memories of good times and good friends being evoked. He also describes the gun fondly, like an old friend – or at least the way I think most friends hope to be remembered – as a friend who "never let him down."

Image 5.13: Hawken 50 Caliber Muzzleloader, Marlin Model 25, 22 Magnum Rifle, and 50 Caliber H & R Sidekick Muzzleloader (from top to bottom).

Guns as Cathartic

Many observations revealed guns owners using guns to cling to something they held dear, whether memories or values, as discussed in the preceding section. There is, however, another category of gun-related ritual that serves the polar opposite function of enabling the gun owner or operator to hold fast to something: the release or emotional purging that comes with the firing of a gun that many report finding cathartic. I made the connection to firing guns and catharsis fairly early on in the data gathering process, when an instructor at the Ohio State Highway Patrol Academy commented that whenever he took groups of cadets out to the firing range, he could "actually see the stress and tension leaving their faces," that it was "always cathartic for them after a stressful day or week." I encountered this phenomenon at each live shooting event that I attended. Recall the account of the woman who exclaimed "happiness is a warm gun" with a big smile on her face at the conclusion of her event with the Scioto Territory Desperados. She had the look of someone who was indeed satisfied and at total peace. Another good example of this type of ritual gun use unfolded prominently at the "Shoot Your Textbook Day" hosted by Ohio University's Second Amendment Club. Image 5.14 below is a copy of a flier circulated to advertise one of the Clubs' "Shoot Your Textbook" days. At this event, I spoke with a wide range of target shooters, all university students with the exception of the NRA representatives onsite for training and instruction. Although it was a rainy day, in the two hours that I was in attendance, I counted 58 students in attendance (40 male and 18 female). The students assembled at a University firing range a few miles away from campus at high noon, in true cowboy fashion. Although the event organizers had some targets set up on the range when we arrived (traditional paper targets and bowling pens), the majority of the students showed up with book in hand and ready to let the book "have it" (see image 5.15). When the event was first brought to my attention, the thought of shooting books brought images of nazi-esque book burnings to mind. However, after speaking with event organizers and attendees alike, it was clear that no one at this event was trying to make a statement about the censorship of reading materials. Some explained to me that "shooting the books" was meant to send a "powerful statement" to local bookstores with unfair practices related to buying books back. For them, it was a release to pull the triggers and obliterate something that they associated with unfair treatment (see image 5.16). The use of the gun, the ultimate power symbol seemed a reasonable way to send a message of disdain. Another form a cathartic release came from students who were shooting books in order to shoot a bad class experience and blast its memory out of existence.

One student commented that she selected her target book, an anthropology text, because "it was a required purchase and the professor never lectured out of it." Another student brought a calculus textbook to shoot after having to take the class three times before passing it. Other people had simply stepped onto the firing range to see what it was like to "squeeze the trigger," or because they "loved to shoot." Whatever the reason, it is clear that emotions of varying type and degree are released on firing ranges as guns are discharged. It should be noted, however, that the cathartic release accompanying the discharging of a gun does not necessarily exist separately from the cathexis other gun owners have achieved through their guns. A gun may house a variety of precious memories held near and dear to a gun owner, who also find it to be an emotional, stress or tension release to pull the trigger.

Image 5.14: Advertisement for Ohio University's Second Amendment Club – Shoot Your Text Book Days.

Image 5.15: "Shoot Your Textbook Day" Targets (books in foreground)

Image 5.16: "Shoot Your Textbook Day" Event in Progress

Gun Cleaning: A Private Ritual

Up to this point, the ritual behavior discussed has focused on a type of public ritual behavior, in that they are ritual activities in which the gun owner shares the gun or experience, openly, with an audience. There exists, however, at least one prominent ritual among gun owners wherein the ritual behavior appears to be a personal matter; and, although visible, at times, to a social audience, the recipient of all ritual deference appears to be only the gun and the precious qualities (ex. memories, freedom, faithful service, loyalty, etc.) that it represents to the handler.

I had noticed in the more than twenty years that I spent as a working musician that guitarists will often take a great deal of care to meticulously clean their instruments after each session. Similarly, most of the professional rodeo athletes that I have interviewed for other research endeavors, like nine time All-Around World Champion Cowboy and bull-riding icon Ty Murray, have also taken great pride and care in preserving their equipment for sustained use. This stands to reason, as instruments, like guns and professional athletic equipment can be very costly. Keeping them clean just ensures career longevity and performance. With gun collectors, however, I observed something going far beyond the simple cleaning of a tool, or even the care of something appreciated. Time and time again, as gun collectors were regaling me with the stories of their guns and what their separate guns mean to them, as the guns were being discussed, the owners held them so gently, as if caressing a babe in arms – holding them the way one might hold something believed to be the most precious thing on earth and the only one of its kind.

In addition to caressing their favorite guns in such a loving manner, I also noticed that they would also clean their guns while they talked – sometimes just lightly with a small and thin cloth cleaning patch, but frequently in a detailed, elaborate, ritual manner. This tendency was not only observed one-on-one with gun collectors who were sharing their stories, however, but also in the field, at the live shooting events. After completing a tournament round, the most common tendency among the participants was to immediately spend some one-on-one time cleaning their guns – often using a portable gun station or bin as depicted in images 5.2 and 5.4).

For most of us, images evoked by the word cleaning are both unpleasant and undesirable. And, to be sure, not all cleaning associated with guns and gun use is taken on with the same zeal and relish. However, for those cleaning a favorite gun – tantamount to a best friend or perhaps something even more precious to some – there was indescribable pride and joy present, and intimate affections shared by the demeaned gun owner with the gun as extreme recipient of deferential treatment. The following is a general compilation of cleaning rituals that I observed unfolding in the field.

As the cleaning began, my gun owners typically started by producing an Outers brand cleaning kit. These and other kits that I observed included a sectional aluminum cleaning rod (the rods used are for the specific caliber and barrel diameter of the gun to be cleaned), a bottle of cleaning solvent (or prolix lubricants), one or two bottles of gun oil, cloth cleaning patches, tips that hold the cleaning patches, and a coarse tool called a bore brush. Although I did not see them in all of the kits used, some included gun grease, a "bore light" to make it easier to see throughout the barrel and breach, and an additional shotgun cleaning accessories called a bore swab and in place of light, oiled rags, a light silicone cloth. As one informant explained "the silicone cloths are for when you want to give the gun a little special lovin'. They keep the fingerprints off and prevent rust better than those old rags." As they sit, carefully eyeballing their guns, the owners either lovingly apply the solvent or lubricant spray- carefully working it through the cylinder chambers and up and down the barrel, inside and out, paying particular care to remove any gunpowder residue/deposit known as "fouling."

The part of the cleaning that always interested me the most was the cleaning of the inside of the barrels. This was achieved by either running the cleaning rod and attached cloths repeatedly through the barrel until it was clean; or, as I observed often in the cleaning of rifle and shotgun barrels, the use of a bore solvent and pipe cleaner-like product called a "bore snake." These products look something like a wide pipe cleaner, several feet in length. They are inserted through the breach and fed through the end of the barrel. After the guns have been silently and carefully inspected, inside and out, gazing up and down the barrel and throughout the chambers, once it meets approval, either a type of dry coating protective lubricant is applied, or the gun oil. This final coating is dabbed with painstaking tenderness until it is evenly applied and the residue shine is minimal.

It is clear that there are "celebrating" and "presentation" elements involved in these cleaning rituals; but, as to the intimate and private aspects of the ritual, there are also aspects of pure deferential appreciation and loving respect being paid to these guns as revealed through the servant-like demeanor of the individuals carrying out the rite. Why was so much visible love and respect going into the cleaning of these pieces of wood and metal if not for show? The details supplied by my informants suggest that this private, intimate ritual of cleaning favorite guns is an affirmation of both cartharsis and cathexis. One informant revealed a commonly-expressed sentiment about cleaning as catharsis in stating that "on cold and rainy days I like to clean my guns and fuss over them. They bring me a sense of peace." It's a stress release because it is a peaceful activity, and one not typically expected to be done in a crowd – something that requires attention and focus. Still, another respondent spoke more of a cathexis-based motivation when he mentioned that he liked to sit alone and clean some of the guns that had been passed down from his grandfather, to his father and then to him. "My grandfather is no longer living, and my father's health is not so great these days. Sitting here, cleaning these guns is kind of like traveling back in time…to good memories with them at their best."

There is one aspect of the gun cleaning ritual that is by no means a private ritual and has nothing to do with cathexis or sentimental gun values. It is possibly a type of catharsis, of sorts, for the cleaner of the gun, however. This type of gun cleaning ritual involves an activity mentioned in the section on guns in popular music and popular culture, and appears to have more to do with the presenting of the gun as a warning than the actual cleaning. It is the intentional, deliberate, highly visible use of gun cleaning as part of the dating ritual. This is not a ritual for just any date. It involves a boy picking up a girl for their first date. During the course of picking the girl up, the scenario requires that the boy meet and receive a speech from the girl's father while he just happens to be cleaning a gun. Whether the display is serious or not, it overtly states "I'm here, with this gun, and ready to use it if you harm that girl." This type of ritual has been celebrated in song, and was also mentioned by a couple of my collectors. One collector counted a gun related to this dating ritual among his favorites. He explained that the Colt .357 magnum revolver was one of his favorites because "this is reported to be the gun my grandfather was "cleaning" in the living room when my father picked up my mother for their first date. The value is purely sentimental: I really have little interest in this type of firearms because it is not military and not good for target shooting. Still I value this above most in my collection because of the story associated with it." Interestingly, in this case, although the grandfather had used the gun a generation earlier as a form of cathexis related to his daughter dating, it went on to be a source of cathexis, an item to be held close and cherished by another.

As the preceding ritual examples demonstrate, guns are directly used as props to facilitate social interactions involving a variety òf emotions, values and activities. Further, these interactions include a series of complementary, integrated deference and demeanor components. Even looking back to the bumper stickers observed at the start of this chapter, the components of deference and demeanor permeate the gun world. The simple act of the Mercedes driver showing up at the gun event displaying a bumper sticker with a gun-related message included equal aspects of deference and demeanor. In deference to guns, the car owner went out of his/her way to prominently display a pro-gun message on a very expensive automobile. The demeanor of the car owner is, at least in part, tied to the message itself: "Ted Kennedy's Car has Killed More People Than my Gun." The simple message reveals the demeanor of a gun enthusiast with a sense of humor, most likely not inclined to vote as a democrat, and openly reverent toward his own "gun."

Personally, I think that the greatest potential application value of identifying the presence of deference and demeanor components in motion and their functions rests on an observation made by Goffman himself. Goffman (1967) argued that we are socially evolving in such a way as to continually do away with more higher powers, and present ourselves in more of a deity-esque light. He also noted, however, that in our current state of social evolution, it is not considered socially appropriate to offer deference to ourselves.

Instead, we must receive deference from others, as deserved from our level of demeanor, and as socially responsive feedback from our social audiences based on the deference we are seen bestowing on the individuals, objects and ideals in receipt of our active recognition. So although it may be considered vulgar for us to praise ourselves, it is not, however, counter to an established moral order to enact appropriate enough "humble" demeanor to convince our social audience that something like a special gun is worth of praise. The appropriately-demeaned individual is then in position to receive praise of the gun and him/herself, for the beauty, special qualities, or wise acquisition of the gun. In the end, the individual has still, in effect, asked a social audience for praise and received it. The process is just channeled through a gun and facilitated by an intricate web of deference and demeanor-based acts.

I must note, however, that although I did witness appropriately demeaned gun owners talking up their guns instead of themselves directly, there were also several instances wherein it was not the presenter that appeared to be seeking praise for themselves (through the praise of their gun's special qualities), but seeking praise for someone else special to them that they associated with the gun. So although Goffman's claim about turning ourselves into little deities, in an interactional sense, does appear to have some merit, here we also have the Durkhemian turning of the gun into something awe inspiring as well as something new: the gun (as object) being used to achieve an acknowledgement and awe inspiring status for others. In a sense, by studying the ways in which deference and demeanor are used in a context as simple as a gun event, we have an opportunity to gauge changes in subtle but important interaction rules, and track our social evolutionary progress. Monitoring and tracking social interaction changes, in general, is too mammoth an undertaking to be practical or useful. Tracking changes to interaction rules within specific contexts, such as gun culture, is feasible. It would be a fairly simple, but long and drawn-out process of tracking changes in self-deference granting over time. In other words, we would be able to address questions about our progress as a people in asking questions such as: are we moving toward a reduced need to seek deferential treatment from others by enacting elaborate demeanor exercises, and entering a new phase of social evolution permissive of self-love and self-deference?

CHAPTER VI

Management of Suspect Identities

Although the preceding chapter focuses on ritual categories observed at gun events and among gun owners and users, there was one special type of ritualistic behavior observed within gun culture that was so dominant that I thought it deserving of its own chapter. This special type of ritual behavior centers on the management of suspect identities. While speaking with my informants on this project, it was far more common than not for the subjects to acknowledge or reference some aspect of the stigma associated with gun ownership. This chapter explores the acknowledgement of stigma, reactions to it, and even, at times, efforts to trade on or cash in the stigma for a perceived social reward.

Many people would question the sanity or moral character of someone who own or collects guns. Consider, for instance, the following gun collector's story of what he felt was an all-too-common experience:

> A while back, my brother had his girlfriend over to meet me. Somehow over the course of the evening, the subject of my gun collection came up. I took them down into the basement, where I keep the vault with some of my favorite guns. Some of my military collection includes guns owned by both Japanese and Nazi soldiers. She was already looking at me different when she saw my guns, like I was creepy or something. I know some people feel uncomfortable around guns, because they think that we're (gun owners) all a bunch of freaks. But when she saw that some of my weapons were Nazi weapons, she wasn't just looking at me like she thought I

was weird, she looked terrified... She said she couldn't believe that I had that kind of stuff, guns and war items, and she made my brother take her home. . .She never really warmed up to me after that.

Recounting his experience, he concluded, "It's just easier to not let people know about my gun stuff. . . You never know when someone is going to react like that."

Another subject who is an Ohio State Trooper shared the following:

On more than one occasion, while I was still living alone in an apartment, I would keep my work gun and belt close to the front door... People would come by sometimes trying to get me to buy things or fill out surveys.... I remember a few different women commenting on the guns when I opened the door, saying things like "what's with the gun?," or "doesn't it make you uncomfortable to have a gun sitting out like that?" They always looked very uncomfortable, like they were looking at some sort of monster, until I put them at easy by explaining that I had the gun because I was an officer. I remember one of them commenting that it (the gun) was just "scary looking."

As the preceding vignettes illustrate, to be a gun collector or enthusiast is, at least frequently, to be cast in a suspect light, or in Everett Hughes' (1945) terms, to be placed in a master status associated with undesirable auxiliary traits. For the gun collector or enthusiast, a maladjusted, "creepy" man gruesomely fascinated with the morbid tools of death.

As I have indicated throughout this project, academic treatments of gun-owning subcultures are sparse and unbalanced. Gun ownership research, for instance, has focused primarily on the demographics of gun ownership and the symbolic value of guns in the American ideology of self-defense and preservation (Squires 2000 and Jiobu and Curry 2001), or the characterization of dealers as anything ranging from art dealers to junk or death brokers (Stenross 1994). None of the extant social science literature on these groups has examined issues of stigmatization and stigma management.

However, as the vignettes with which this section began demonstrate, issues of stigma management are significant features of the social landscapes of this subculture. This became apparent while studying gun shows and repeatedly encountering social psychological challenges and engaging in stigma management techniques that have been reported across a range of other social groups, as well. In this chapter, I present an ethnographic analysis of in-group stigma management in which I draw upon concepts from previous research on stigma management to illuminate aspects of the social worlds of gun collectors that have not previously received analytic scrutiny. In turn, the findings expand and enhance empirical and conceptual treatments of this generic social process (Prus 1996).

A key tenet of ethnographic research is that the researcher's "fieldwork role" or position vis-à-vis the group influences the kinds of data and perspectives he or she will be able to access. This would seem to be especially the case in relation to such audience-sensitive topics as stigma management. In comparing the fieldwork roles and "informational yield" (Snow et al. 1986) associated with the group discussed in this chapter, I find that the more "peripheral membership role" (Adler and Adler 1987: 32-37) used, not surprisingly, yielded significantly more stigma management data related to out-group interactions. In particular, the initial stages of interviews frequently included defensive efforts by individuals to portray themselves as "normal," in spite of their affiliations with gun culture. At the same time, interviewees also often lashed out with statements of distrust or rejection of outsiders, including academic researchers. At such moments the researcher was particularly sensitized to the importance of convincingly presenting himself as a "sympathetic" outsider who was truly interested in the views and experiences of group members.

While the foregoing informational biases were evident in relation to the primary fieldwork roles used in this project, the study was pursued with an eye toward achieving empirical and theoretical saturation (Charmaz 2006; Glaser 2001; Lofland et al. 2005) of relevant analytic categories. Further, I have sought, when possible and appropriate, to move across different observational roles (e.g., as audience members at gun shows or as a formal student at a gun shooting event) in order to gain a broader set of data and analytic sensitivities. As a result, I am confident in the general scope and depth of the data, especially in regards to the topic of this chapter.

While I have witnessed the frequent reluctance of members of this subculture to talk with non-peers (including at times, the novice insider), I have also found that once I was able to establish rapport with members of these groups, they often became quite enthusiastic and forthcoming. As Anderson and Calhoun (1992) noted, members of deviant groups frequently enjoy uncritical attention and interest, and may warm up nicely to the chance to "tell their story" once they feel confident in the researcher's genuine interest. Such has certainly been my experience with gun owners and enthusiasts.

STIGMATIZATION

Stigmatization, to one degree or another, is widespread throughout American society. Indeed, part of what has made Goffman's *Stigma* such an influential work is the applicability of many of his concepts to a broad swath of humanity. Still, the extent and intensity of stigma vary considerably among social groups and individuals. It is important, therefore, to substantiate the claim that gun collectors perceive themselves, and are perceived by others, as stigmatized or deviant groups.

Consider first the case of gun collectors who commonly perceive themselves as negatively characterized by the media. In summarizing media treatments of gun owners and issues in general, Bane (2001) has documented the dominance of pejorative portrayals. Some of the findings he cites come directly from complaints from pro-gun constituencies, as in claims from the Media Research Center, a conservative media watchdog group, that during a two-year period in the late 1990s, the ratio of anti-gun to pro-gun stories on major television networks ran almost 10 to one in favor of gun control (19). The biggest "offender," they report, was ABC's *Good Morning America*, which ran 92 anti-gun stories and only one pro-gun story. More academically-oriented studies have also found a predominance of negative portrayals of, and attitudes toward, gun-groups in the mainstream media, as in Patrick's (1999) report that the National Rifle Association was portrayed negatively in editorial and op-ed pieces 87 percent of the time. Not surprisingly, gun collectors lament what they feel is an unbalanced caricature of gun culture and gun owner values. At the same time, however, other images of guns, the images of the cool cowboy, heroic soldier, and police officer, also permeate the cable channels and movie screens. This sets guns up to be something both stigmatized and desirable – depending on the social context.

Gun owners also tend to see academic researchers as harboring "liberal agendas" and negative attitudes that find their way into print. Throughout the course of his study, the investigator was consistently reminded that "reporters," including social science researchers, were viewed with distrust. Some informants shared personal accounts of how they had been mislead by previous researchers who came to them with the promise of neutrality toward the issue of gun ownership, only to later depict the same gun owners in a less-than-favorable light. As one research subject who is a member of the NRA, PRO (Peoples Rights Organization) and OGCA (Ohio Gun Collector's Association) explained:

> There are some of your questions that I won't answer, simply for security reasons. I am not surprised you aren't getting much response from OGCA members. Most tend to be wary of those they don't know. Too often reporters or academics have used this type of information, out of context, to paint Gun Collectors as extremist or nut cases. The OGCA is about the nicest group of people you will ever meet, but many won't be comfortable opening up to you until you gain their trust, and they know your motivations.

As the foregoing discussion illustrates, gun owners are well aware that many people look on their activities as deviant. Still, members of these groups do not simply accept stigma and the devalued selves it implies. Rather, like members of other stigmatized groups, they routinely engage in activities directed toward managing their interactions with others in order to mitigate negative stereotypes or at least to minimize the application of those stereotypes to them personally. The following is an exploration of this type of activity.

MANAGING STIGMA

In his classic work on stigma management, Goffman (1963) distinguished between out-group strategies that are used in interactions with those who are outside the stigmatized group and in-group strategies that are used to soften stigma in interaction with one's peers.

In this chapter, the primary focus is on out-group stigma management, as it was encountered the most heavily, with additional considerations of in-group strategies, as well. The goal of out-group stigma management strategies is to avoid being perceived as morally or socially flawed by virtue of one's identification with a particular stigmatized status or activity. In-group stigma strategies are an extension of the same subject. However, instead of working to avoid detection and negative treatment from society at large, in-group strategies involve a type of mutual support that similarly situated (in terms of being the recipient of stigmatization) peers provide to one another to cope with their stigma. One key aspect of successful stigma management is strategic control over what information is revealed to, or withheld from, non-peers. A second dimension of out-group stigma management involves providing an interpretive frame within which potentially stigmatizing information is either neutralized or presented in a positive light. Both of these orientations toward out-group stigma management play important roles in the social activities of gun collectors. In the following discussion I begin by examining two kinds of individualized strategies, one directed toward information control and the other involving verbal techniques for defining one's identity and activities in non-stigmatizing ways. Next, two forms of collective out-group stigma management are addressed, one of which emphasizes the dramatic countering of stigmatizing stereotypes while the other focuses on creating positive associations and connotations for the gun collectors' identities and activities.

INDIVIDUAL STIGMA MANAGEMENT STRATEGIES

Passing and Avoidance

The strategy of passing involves "the management of undisclosed discrediting information about self" (Goffman 1963:42). While successful passing may require substantial effort on the part of those whose stigma is readily apparent, for gun collectors it is relatively simple, often involving little more than avoiding disclosing one's avocational identity and activities to others.

The gun collector's story at the start of this paper about his brother's girlfriend's hostility toward him once she saw his guns makes it understandable why gun collectors would engage in information control to limit others' awareness of their activity. Still, like other stigmatized groups reported in the literature (e.g., Schneider and Conrad 1980; Herman 1993; Thorne and Anderson 2006), gun collectors reported that their efforts to pass involved "selective concealment." In particular, gun collectors often mentioned their residential neighbors and their co-workers as audiences from whom it was important to withhold information about their potentially stigmatizing activities. So, for instance, a Cleveland-area gun collector and car salesman explained,

> My neighbors have no idea about what's in this vault (gun safe), and I don't want them to find out. This is a pretty quiet neighborhood, and we try to help one another out when we can, but people around here can really talk some shit about each other. The last thing I need is people running around saying that I'm some kind of gun nut, with my neighbors thinking that I'm going to go on some kind of rampage.

Yet another interviewee, a southeast Ohio accountant, spoke of his desire to keep his gun collecting hidden from his co-workers. Using his experience with his religious activities as an analogy, he explained,

> When I'm ... around other collectors or shooters at a tournament or show, I get into it as much as anyone. I have no problem with anyone there knowing that I'm a gun owner. I'm proud to be one. When it comes to people I work with, it's kind of like church. If you're in church on Sunday, you have nothing to hide about your religion when you are there with those people, worshiping the same thing . .. There you are safe. With your guns, if you are with other gun people at a show, you are safe to be enthusiastic about guns and sing their praises. Now I'm not going to go around my office trying to convert my co-workers to my religion. They might think I'm a freak for doing that just the same as they would if I told that about my guns. It's just not worth the risk.

In addition to avoiding stigma, gun collectors often feel that hiding their gun collecting serves another purpose as well. Since the guns in their collections may range in monetary value up to $10,000 and more, gun collectors may see it as unwise to publicize the fact that such guns are stored in their homes. "We might as well just yell out 'Come and get it!'" said one informant. Indeed, the combination of fear of stigmatization and security issues leads many gun collectors to be secretive and distrustful.

My findings that gun collectors engage in passing behavior provides one glimpse into their efforts to manage the stigma they experience. Yet passing is not always either possible or acceptable. For one thing, unlike deviant "loners," such as the self-injurers studied by Adler and Adler (2005), gun collectors must pursue their goals through social activities. While self-injurers can act in isolation, gun collecting requires co-participants. Further, a significant part of the pleasure and motivation of gun collecting lies in a degree of social recognition associated with the avowal of these specific avocational identities, both from peers and non-peers. Even though many outsiders may view gun collecting as suspect activities, there are other, more curious, outsiders who are open to seeing these activities in a positive light. Being a completely closeted gun collector, even if it were possible, would dramatically limit one's opportunities to reach out to non-peers who might be recruited to the activities or at least show an interest in them. By virtue of this, gun collectors find themselves interacting with non-peers, and managing their potential stigmatization in those encounters. The other kinds of stigma management discussed in this section are all directed specifically toward actively managing interactions with non-peers.

Disclaimers and Techniques of Neutralization

When individuals face stigma in interactions with others, they often invoke verbal techniques to justify or explain their untoward behaviors of conditions in ways they hope will mitigate their stigmatization. Sociologists have examined the use of many different kinds of overlapping rhetorical strategies in managing stigma, including vocabularies of motive (Mills 1940), techniques of neutralization (Sykes and Matza 1957), accounts (Scott and Lyman 1968), and disclaimers (Hewitt and Stokes 1975). Among gun collectors I found disclaimers and techniques of neutralization to be particularly common.

As Hewitt and Stokes conceptualized disclaimers, they are statements made to ward off the imputation of deviance in the face of forthcoming problematic actions or information. The use of disclaimers was frequently observed in the gun collector research. Most often, disclaimers were offered at the very beginning of an interview, as interviewees sought to distance themselves at the outset from deviant stereotypes of gun collectors. So, for example, one informant prefaced his interview by stating, "Before we begin, I would just like you to know that I'm not a freak. I don't want to start a militia or anything." As the preceding quote reveals, such disclaimers do not necessarily deny the existence of the stereotypical deviant, but rather, seek to establish the respectability of the individual him- or herself. This point is further illustrated by another interviewee who explained his interest in gun collecting by saying, "I'm just collecting history here," while quickly adding, "I'm not one of those weirdoes that you hear about on the news."

Another kind of verbal response to potential stigmatization involves what Gresham Sykes and David Matza (1957) refer to as techniques of neutralization. Techniques of neutralization were originally conceived by Sykes and Matza as cognitive rationalizations that enabled individuals to overcome potential moral constraints, thus facilitating their participation in deviant acts. But it is widely acknowledged today (e.g., Cromwell and Thurman 2003) that techniques of neutralization also serve as forms of stigma management, providing explanations and "accounts" (Scott and Lyman 1968) that justify suspect or questionable behavior. Members of the subcultures reported in this paper commonly invoked three particular techniques of neutralization: "denial of injury," "appeal to higher loyalties," and "condemnation of the condemners."

Among gun collectors, the most pervasive technique of neutralization was "denial of injury." A full 90 percent of the study population went out of their way (often before the interview questions had even begun), to assert that their guns were not harming anyone. A case in point is that of a building contractor from central Ohio who commented,

> I know that guns are used as weapons to kill people every day. Those aren't my guns. The world is safe from my collection. I own over 100 guns. Some of them have been in my family for over 120 years. To my knowledge, none of them have ever been used for anything other than sport.

In using an appeal to higher loyalties, individuals make verbal claims that their deviance is not in fact deviant, but rather, that it represents their commitment to more important responsibilities and values. Most gun collectors framed the purpose of their collection in the context of a higher loyalty that made collecting guns not only understandable in their eyes, but a moral responsibility. For some that loyalty was to their family and its history. As one subject described this connection, "With part of my collection, I'm carrying the torch for my family. Some of the people who owned these guns are dead. All that I have left of them is their memories and these guns. . . Now you take away these guns, you're taking away memories." The most common invocation of higher loyalty among gun collectors, however, was to a broader national "right to bear arms" and the recognition of sacrifices that have been made to maintain this tradition. As another informant explained his commitment to gun collecting, "We seem to forget that people literally died to give us the right to own these guns."

The "condemning of condemners" can also serve to justify one's own suspect behavior by pointing out the moral failures and inconsistencies of those who would demean that behavior. The condemnations directed toward condemners may challenge opponents for failing to embrace the loyalties to which stigmatized individuals are themselves deeply committed. An excellent example of this was provided by the gun collector above who explicitly linked his gun collecting with people who "died to give us the right to own these guns." Lashing out at those who oppose gun ownership, this collector angrily asked, "Are we supposed to piss on the freedom they gave us just because the occasional jack ass doesn't lock up his piece?" Implicit in his comment is the assertion that those who oppose gun ownership are, indeed, disrespectfully "pissing" on that freedom. Even the researcher in this study, by virtue of being an academic, and therefore an assumed "liberal," found himself at times being the focus of direct condemnation, such as that captured in the words of an interviewee who told him, "You liberals just want to take away our heritage. I'm more of a true American than most people. How far back can you trace your ancestry? I've had relatives here since the 1500s. Can you say that?"

COLLECTIVE STIGMA MANAGEMENT STRATEGIES

The stigma management practices discussed so far in this paper are techniques that are used by individuals. At times, however, stigma management can take a collective turn, with members of a stigmatized group working together to manage the impressions that others have of them. The next section is an examination of such collective strategies to challenge discrediting images and perceptions.

Dramaturgical Stereotype Busting

The first type of collective stigma management explored is what I refer to as "dramaturgical stereotype busting." This form of stigma management involves a staged or dramatized performance designed to counter negative stereotypical notions of relevant types of people and activities. Gun subcultures have displays and performances that dramatize concerns that are designed to challenge stereotypes of them. Given public beliefs about the dangers associated with guns, many of the stereotype busting displays and performances of these groups are explicitly directed toward highlighting their attention to safety.

Examples of dramaturgical stereotype busting were highly visible at the two dozen gun shows that the researcher attended in Ohio and Texas. Each show, without exception, promoted regional safety issues, relevant gun laws, and community awareness. At NRA and PRO gun events, for instance, promotional displays and handouts consistently included publicity and sign-up forms for local courses that provide training in various safety techniques. It is also common for NRA events to display materials from their Eddie Eagle GunSafe® Program directed toward children in pre-kindergarten through third grade. This program offers a curriculum with instructional materials, workbooks, and an animated video featuring the "Eddie Eagle" mascot to schools interested in teaching the program. As illustrated in image 6.1 below, Bumper decals and student reward stickers prominently proclaim the four simple rules for children who find a gun: **"STOP! Don't Touch. Leave the Area. Tell an Adult."** The following image is of a lapel sticker collected by the researcher at a gun show in Columbus, Ohio.

Image 6.1: NRA GunSafe® Program Eddie the Eagle Student Reward Sticker.

As their promotional materials explain, "Just as Smokey Bear teaches children not to play with matches, Eddie Eagle teaches them that firearms should not be touched" (National Rifle Association 2008).

Here we observe gun collectors acknowledging the potential reality of gun-related dangers and presenting themselves as extremely serious promoters of safety while at the same time embracing gun rights and ownership. Dramaturgical stereotype busting is even more dramatically enacted in many gun club activities in which many gun collectors participate. In gun clubs with "live action" role players, for instance, there are explicit safety rules that are often read aloud not only at the start of the day's activities, but prior to each specific shooting event. Among the safety rules that are consistently repeated at each event in Cowboy Action Shooting matches sponsored by SASS (the Single Action Shooting Society) are the following:

1. Treat and respect every firearm at all times as if it were loaded.

2. Muzzle direction is important between, before, during, and after shooting a stage. . . Failure to manage safe muzzle direction is grounds for disqualification.

3. All firearms shall remain unloaded except when under the direct observation of a Range Officer on the firing line or in the loading area.

4. No cocked revolver may ever leave a shooter's hand.

5. Once a revolver is cocked, the round under the hammer must be expended in order for it to be returned to a safe condition. (Single Action Shooting Society 2008)

The highly visible and repetitive ritual in which these rules are publicly pronounced serves as a dramaturgical display to counter negative stereotypes. Further, not only are the rules read aloud at the start of each shooting event, but they are often closely enforced, as in the case spotters who are posted directly behind the shooter with orders to disarm any shooter who violates the "170 Degree Rule" that stipulates that gun muzzles must always be pointing down range from any possible audience.. According to official SASS rules, movement directly toward the crowd with a loaded firearm is to be interpreted as an unexpected and dangerous act of aggression and hostility. Spotters positioned behind shooters in the staging areas are typically on hand to "disarm" anyone who violates this rule. As one shooter at a tournament in Chillicothe, Ohio emphatically told the researcher,

> We recognize that the average person will assume that we are reckless, dangerous, and either likely to get hurt or hurt others. For this reason, we take safety and safety precautions very seriously. Anyone violating the 170 degree or other safety rules will be escorted, by the group, to the entrance and permanently banned. Participants who are reckless with their guns, or are anything but serious around here, are in no way welcome!

In highlighting the ways in which the foregoing activities serve as public relations performances, I do not mean to suggest that they are merely public relations strategies. The activities described here are not just window dressing; they are directed to real safety concerns. None of the gun collectors in my study denied the risk of serious harm or death associated with their avocational interests. Indeed, members of these groups have developed the activities discussed here specifically to reduce those risks. But, especially in their more public forms, these activities also carry expressive implications about who gun collectors are—that they are not irresponsible risk-takers, but may in fact be as vigilant, or more vigilant, about safety than are most of the people who would criticize them.

Transcendence and Idiosynchracy Credit

Destigmatization is a term developed by Carol Warren (1980) to refer to ways in which those who are openly known as members of a stigmatized group may overcome their definition as deviant. One particular form of destigmatization is what Warren calls transcendence, where members of a stigmatized group "rise above" the deviant stereotypes of "people like them." I am interested in collective stigma management that involves members of the groups I have studied, and how they might work together in order to achieve destigmatization.

One particular form of destigmatizating transcendence that I have repeatedly observed throughout this study is associated with the building of what Hollander (1958) termed "idiosyncrasy credit"—a process through which a morally suspect individual or group improves their reputation through some form of community service and association with a "good cause." Just as David Snow (1979) found that Nichiren Shoshu Buddhists sought to enhance their reputation through visible association with well-regarded causes and values, I find similar activities among gun people. The Ohio Gun Collectors Association, for instance, has organized its Disabled Shooting Championship and various youth outreach programs both as a way to increase interest in gun-oriented activities and to demonstrate its commitment to broader civic responsibilities. Gun and shooting clubs also frequently use events to raise money for specific causes, such as breast cancer and multiple sclerosis research or for college scholarships. Among the most widely publicized charity causes that has been organized in recent years is "Sugarbugs Celebrity Shoot," a clay target shooting event features various celebrities and politicians and raises money for the treatment of childhood diabetes. An article on WomenandGuns.com summarizes the event, by proclaiming, "Celebrities, politicians, shooters, guns, targets, and a good cause. What better way is there to spend a weekend?" The importance of the public relations component of such events is captured in the words of a gun club participant in his description of the resounding success of a large annual SASS called the End of the Trail. "The event," he reported, "received local and national news coverage and there even were television crews from Europe and Japan." He continued:

> To top it off, End of Trail donated $10,000 of the match proceeds to the Roy Rogers and Dale Evans Happy Trails Children's Foundation. In all, End of Trail has donated more than $100,000 to the organization. You can't buy this type of positive press which benefits the entire shooting industry (Huntington 1997).

By associating themselves with humanitarian concerns, gun collectors present themselves as "more than" just hobbyists involved in their respective subcultures. In showing their altruism and social responsibility, they present yet further evidence to counter stigmatizing stereotypes of them.

IN GROUP STRATEGIES

As previously mentioned, as an outsider of the gun world, I was far more likely to directly experience stigma management strategies that were applied to outsiders (i.e. me and other outsiders discussed by my informants) than those in group strategies shared among similarly (in terms of relative stigma) situated gun collectors. The following entails my direct observations pertaining to in group strategies to which I was privy as an observer and passive participant.

Normalizing Fear

As noted by many of my research subjects, gun enthusiasts are well aware of the primary images of horror associated with gun ownership by the nay sayers:

Kids with guns scare the shit out of people.
If you're going to arm the morons, you have to arm everyone.

Similar sentiments were shared by the overwhelming majority of the research subjects when discussing the perceived concerns of the opposition. Interestingly, major proponents of gun ownership, including the nation's two largest gun advocacy groups (NRA and PRO), popular trade publications, and even some of the large live action gun clubs have organized around these issues, and in some ways even profiting directly from these public concerns and sources of stigmatization. Starting with the first issue addressed – the concern over children coming into contact with firearms – the general response to this issue might appear counter-intuitive at first glance. However, upon close scrutiny, the rhyme and reason are unveiled. The NRA and PRO have responded to the first two issues listed above by essentially saying it's all about the safety. If kids with guns scare you, then train them how to use guns properly (make sure that you are trained first), be aware of community safety issues, familiarize yourself with gun laws, and use some common sense to ensure that anything dangerous is properly secured/locked-up. Further, if you or anyone else comes across a situation involving guns that are dangerous, report it. These values are heavily promoted in PRO and NRA publications and gun show literature. In general, safety and inclusion are two of the most ever-present scenes at their gun events. Instead of buckling to public pressure to keep guns out of the hands of kids, these organizations say take away the concern through awareness and education. Arm everyone. Arm your family, your wife, kids, everyone who can learn the RIGHT way to handle a gun. Each group promotes a series of events each year the attempt to draw in more families and children. Accordingly, promotional materials (see image 7.1) marketed exclusively for children are circulated at NRA and PRO events. Similarly, large live action shooting clubs, like the Scioto Territory Desperados, actively recruit families and even young children to participate in their shooting events. While visiting the club for the first time, one research subject, a female dental hygienist from central Ohio commented about a 10-year old girl that was shooting that day. "What did you think of her? We know that some folks are a little shocked an uneasy when they come here and see kids this young shooting in a tournament – especially little girls." Not only has this organization embraced the family and children inclusion views espoused by the PRO and NRA, they celebrate it. Pictures of these children shooting rifles and pistols (granted in the most controlled safety environment that I have witnessed in my life) are often proudly displayed on the group's website (http://www.sciotodesperados.com).

Condemning the Condemners

Subculture members who share stigmatized status are often particularly open to demeaning the opposition: condemning those who would condemn the subculture under consideration. Although I have demonstrated how this may be observed directly as an out group management technique, it is also commonly employed as an in group activity. For instance, throughout my field research, I was continually confronted by the anti-liberal sentiment ubiquitous in gun culture. From various accounts from my many informants about how liberals are "out to get their guns" and anti-liberal bumper-sticker rhetoric to t-shirts, liberals are clearly being condemned by the gun collecting audience. They are being condemned for being too weak, blind, cowardly and bleeding-heart to recognize the real dangers they are perpetuating by failing to support gun ownership. Nowhere is this illustrated more clearly than the highly popular rendering of the hippie peace symbol of the 1960s as the "footprint of the American Chicken." This popular t-shirt equates peace with the ultimate form of weakness: being a coward - and not just any coward, an un-American coward. In one of its advertisements to sell the t-shirt, the marketing company Life, Liberty, Etc., has the following to say about those who pick up the peace symbol instead of a gun:

> Often found in dense urban areas, the American Chicken can be identified by its distinctive mark and complete lack of understanding. However, when confronted with heavy caliber truth and large volleys of common sense, they will often retreat back to their hippie communes while ranting incoherently. This t-shirt will help you identify these radical individuals so they can be avoided when possible and confronted when necessary (www.info@lifelibertyetc.com).

This short paragraph is full of so much rich, candid and accurate detail of the sentiment expressed by so many within the world of the gun. Anyone who speaks of peace must not only be a liberal, but the enemy - not only the enemy, but an urban dwelling, stupid enemy that may need to be confronted. Some other examples of popular t-shirts with messages actively condemning those who stand in the way of gun rights that I encountered– and many that you may well notice out there in your daily lives are as follows:

Guns Don't Kill People It's Those Dang Angry Minorities

A Gun In The Hand Is Better Than A Cop On The Phone

100,000,000 Legal Firearm Owners Killed No One Yesterday

I Carry A Gun Because A Cop Is Too Heavy

Be on the lookout. Slogans like these are walking around on human billboards in the form of t-shirts, and are displayed on automobiles in towns all across America. I do not want to misrepresent the truth by stating that most of my informants spoke negatively of society at large, and certainly none among them spoke of any radical desire for any kind of revolution or violence. However, it was very common for the assertion to be made that non-gun folk are cowards and that they are clueless people who are doing more harm than good to society by attempting to disarm it. I've heard the idea expressed a variety of different ways, but the following statement made by a shotgun vendor at a Cleveland-area gun show says it all:

> The idiots don't realize that if you take guns away from law abiding citizens that only the cops and the crooks will be armed.

A highly-animated hunter from Logan, Ohio, who referred to me as a "city boy ," stated the following:

> You people don't want to see me drivin' around with my guns in the truck now. When those terrorists show up again, I bet

you don't think I'm so weird then. Then ya'll want us to take care of you.

Here, not only do we see the pro-active condemning of the condemners once again, but the gun owner aggrandizes himself to be not only on the right side of the issue, but also the savior.

Trading on Stigma

One of the truly magical benefits of conducting research based on the grounded theoretical approach is that the researcher is afforded the opportunity to get out of the way of the data, stand back, and see what unfolds. From the seamless, chaotic yet beautiful ballet of social interaction surrounding gun-related activities, there emerges something unique and noteworthy in the realm of stigmatization. Unlike the typical documented sources of stigmatization, such as mental illness, homelessness, and bankruptcy, which elicit a host of previously discussed management techniques that are also employed by gun enthusiasts, the gun enthusiast has the rare ability to trade on his/her stigmatized identity at will. As previously discussed, stigma management strategies are typically utilized to lessen the negative impact of a denigrated and suspect identity. As demonstrated in the previous sections, in certain social contexts, gun enthusiasts also find it necessary to practice stigma management strategies and fade into the "normal," bland background scenery, when they find themselves at odds with a social audience perceived to be more closely aligned with the moral order. However, there are also clear, observable instances in which the gun enthusiast derives positive social status directly from the negative or stigmatized properties of these unique hobbies.

It is not uncommon for the owner of a gun to base the value of the weapon not only on monetary appraisal, but also on its violent history. For instance, according to a December 27, 1999, article in the New York Times, the 38.-Caliber, snub-nosed Colt Cobra revolver that Jack Ruby used to kill Lee Harvey Oswald was sold for $220,000. The 2008 Official Gun Digest Book of Guns and Prices lists the monetary value for a gun of this type at less than $300 (268). This phenomenon was illuminated by one of my research subjects in a June, 2007, interview. He discussed his passion for "weapons that were used in combat," and noted that he assigned value to the guns based on "how close they made him feel to the action." Among his collection was a Japanese Nambu 8mm pistol (see image 6.2). The subject stated that he had only paid $200 for the pistol. It was a notoriously unreliable gun, and typically not highly valued among collectors.

Although he had guns with estimated values of over $5,000 in his collection, he stated that he considered this gun as one of the most valuable to him because "it had been taken from the body of a dead soldier, so it put him (the collector) directly at the battle scene." The collector liked the idea of a gun that "put him closer to the battle scene." He disclosed that he had supporting evidence that the gun had been taken into battle and that the soldier's life had been cut short based on some wadded up paper that he found in the bottom of the holster.

Image 6.2: Japanese Nambu 8mm Pistol

He said that he had the Japanese Department at The Ohio State University translate what turned out to be the text of an ad for real estate that the soldier was trying to sell. The idea that the ad was never posted, but he knew something about the intimate goings on of the soldier at the time of his death intrigued the collector. I forwarded a copy of the document (see image 6.3) to Dr. Hiroyuki Oshita, Graduate Chair of Linguistics and Professor of Japanese at Ohio University. Dr. Oshita confirmed that the document is indeed a draft of ad copy listing two properties in Naha City, Okinawa. Another example of trading on gun-related stigma was cited by many of the hunters in the sample population. As one of them noted, "I think that the average person is probably pretty disgusted by the idea of the Bambi killer aspect of deer hunting. Most of them would probably be even more disgusted if they knew that me and most of my buddies value our rifles based on performance and accuracy. That means that the more deer that we take or harvest (kill), the more the gun means to us." These two varied accounts suggest that the active trading on suspect identities is, indeed, a part of gun culture. Additionally, this is an area of gun culture that has yet to be researched in any notable way by the academic community.

Image 6.3: Supporting Paperwork of Japanese Nambu 8mm Pistol's Living History

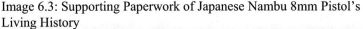

Warrior Narratives and Badassitudes

As was illustrated in the preceding section by the account of the collector who liked the idea of a gun's history putting him "closer to the battle scene," it was a common practice for my informants to engage in a type of warrior narratives - or expressing what I call "badassedness" or "badassitudes" as derived from Katz (1997) in an exploration of badass ways – as a means by which to "trade" on gun stigma with like-stigmatized gun owners and operators.

In chapter two, I explained that warrior narratives are the running scripts lived out by individual social actors that unfold during the course of performing some aspect of masculinity (Jordan and Cowan 2007). Just as Jordan and Cowan (2007) observed warrior narratives used by children in a Kindergarten classroom to negotiate aspects of gender along a variety of basic tasks, leisure activities and general social exchanges, I have continually observed adult gun owners trading warrior narratives surrounding the use of their guns. The guns and stories or accounts about guns are directly traded in to facilitate a perceived aspect of masculinity. The specific aspects of masculinity constructed typically centered around the tough and cool, and paralleled the reflections provided by the male prisoners in Evans and Wallace (2008) study, wherein they persistently encountered narratives including similar themes of "emotional suppression," "hardness," "power," and a need to mask any and all weakness at all times.

The warrior narratives under consideration are very similar to what Mills and Tivers (2001) and Hunt (2008) describe as living histories. These living histories typically refer to past events that are reconstructed through "serious leisure," with a specific place (such as a battlefield) in mind. Hunt has argued that "traditional masculinities" are "negotiated and manufactured" through a "site of a serious leisure pursuit that attempts to draw boundaries with the feminine" (Hunt 2008: 460). Here she is talking about specific sites, such as battlefields, where a known type of masculinity is actively performed, through the leisure of detailed outdoor performance – with an effort to do the masculinity in an historically accurate way. Warrior narratives, interestingly, achieve essentially the same basic ends, with actual research subjects, in real time, providing living narratives surrounding any specific place, activity or aspect of culture (such as a gun) that the researcher is lucky enough to observe. I have maintained through theoretical elaboration and varied observations that guns are ascribed symbolic value based on their living histories. In the case of the gun, it becomes a type of historical site, and I have captured narratives surrounding its use for further analysis below.

The first instance centers on the observations of Tom, an avid central Ohio gun collector who primarily specializes in military guns. While sharing the stories of his guns and what he values about each, one of Tom's stories that really stood out was that of the French Unique "Kriegsmodell" WWII Nazi Occupation 7.65 pistol. According to Tom, the gun was already valuable monetarily, due to only an estimated 18,000 ever having been made. Although he estimated the gun's worth at over $600 USD, it was an unusual and distinctive warrior narrative that added value to the gun in Tom's eyes. "This was not a particularly high-quality or reliable gun, but it's typically worth more than those made by the same manufacturer during other time periods that have a better track record." You'll note that there is a Nazi Army accepted Eagle/WaAD20 stamp on this gun. French workers made this line of guns during the Nazi occupation of France. Worker quality dropped off during the same time. I think this says something amazing about the human spirit and their will and determination. Don't you think? And that's why I consider this one to be among my most valuable. Even as captives, they were fighters in their own way."

In addition to the civilian collector's observations above, there are undeniably special considerations to be afforded soldiers and members of law enforcement agencies who must call upon their trusty arms (or at least the potential is there to do such) in times of high risk and danger, for their preservation or the preservation of those they are sworn to protect and defend. The life of a true warrior might even require the use of a warrior narrative in the course of regular daily life. Irrespective of that fact, the warrior narratives I've observed from non-law enforcement and military personnel, at least in the case of this study, are a close approximation.

> I take some comfort for myself and my wife in knowing that
> my Glock will bring down a large man.

The statement above was made by an Ohio Law Enforcement Officer who was explaining some of the inter-personal difficulties of wearing a gun as part of his work uniform. In addition to people viewing him with "more suspicion" and "acting different towards him" when he "wears the gun," "they react to the gun." But he was more concerned about the impact it had on his wife and family. The gun was a "constant reminder" of the dangers of his job, and he needed to be able to reassure them and himself that he was well-protected by his gun. This is understandable. I have noticed, however, that my hunter informants and other collectors of military weapons use almost identical types of warrior narratives (comments similar to "bring down" a man) in discussing what favorite guns mean to them and sharing their gun stories. It was often the number of kills, or the gun's life history of efficient killing, that gave it its position of prominence within a collection.

> It is a fine shooting gun and I have taken several deer with it.
> I've dropped a lot of big game with that Winchester.
> My dad and I were trying to figure up a count recently, and I'm pretty sure that I've harvested over 40 (deer) with my Thompson. That's why it's one of my favorite.

These accounts taken from among my hunter/collectors are fairly representative of comments to which I was privy at a variety of gun events. The more killing, the more valued the gun that delivered the shot. Note the use of the similar warrior narrative language that was expressed by the officer in the first example of the section. I have "taken;" "I've dropped;" and "I've harvested." These are all expressions used in the world of sport shooters to convey the killing of live game, and mean the same as the officer's comment about being able to "bring down" a man. We are not, of course, talking about something akin to the killing of a man, but the narrative style is almost identical.

The final observations that I have made pertaining to the use of warrior narratives surrounding guns actually comes from the ritual practice of "blooding." I did not include a separate description of blooding in the ritual section, simply because I was focusing on rituals that I believed to be fairly common – and to my knowledge, blooding rituals are not widely practiced. I only encountered the practice as being referenced twice during my data collection, but given the extreme nature of the practice, I thought it worth mentioning. Blooding rituals in gun sports have been referenced in academic literature as far back as

Flugel's (1931) study of Fox Hunting Rites. According to Flugel, the practice of blooding typically involves a first-time hunter who has killed large game, such as deer or a fox. In keeping with the ritual, the hunter who takes the game will either drink a small amount of the animal's blood, bite/eat a small piece of raw flesh or organ, or smear some of the blood on their cheeks (similar to native American war paint). The hunter is then to offer up some sort of barbaric war cry as a sign of their masculinity. Two of my informants shared stories of observed blooding rituals as part of a deer harvest. One informant stated that his uncle and father had him drink a small amount of the deer's blood on the occasion of his first harvest. The other informant was not personally blooded, but he was part of a hunting party wherein one of his friends, a hunter named Brian, was goaded relentlessly by the hunting party until he bit a piece of raw liver that was taken from his first harvested deer. In each case, possibly more relevant than the highly warrior-like ritual involving the eating of raw meat and smearing of animal blood, is that after this ritual was completed, the participants in the group took turns sharing "best of" stories about kills and incredible shots made with their favorite guns. They celebrated their own warrior achievements and qualities, actively embracing them (qualities that would horrify if not repulse much of the general population) by reaffirming the warrior achievements and qualities of their guns.

CONCLUSIONS

In this chapter I have broadened the application of stigma management concepts by demonstrating the relevance of social groups that have not previously been examined from this analytic perspective. I have presented evidence that gun collectors (rightfully) perceive themselves as often subject to stigmatizing public stereotypes. They respond to this stigmatization by adopting a range of strategies to counter or mitigate negative stereotypes in their interaction with others. At the individual level they often try to pass and avoid bringing up their suspect identities and activities. Individuals also invoke verbal disclaimers and techniques of neutralization, prominently including appeals to higher loyalties, denial of injury, and condemning of condemners. At the collective or group level, I identified two other forms of stigma management: dramaturgical stereotype busting and destigmatization through the building of idiosyncrasy credit.

By illustrating the applicability of concepts developed across a wide range of stigma management studies to groups that have not previously been examined from this perspective, my analysis represents what Snow et al. (2003) have referred to as "theoretical extension" in ethnographic research. One clear implication of this section is that the interactionist literature on stigma management may be valuable for illuminating a broader range of social groups than typically recognized. Indeed, this observation is consistent with Goffman's wry (albeit unnecessarily gendered) observation over forty years ago that the only American male free of stigma is the "young, married, white, urban, northern, heterosexual Protestant father of college educated, fully employed, of good complexion, weight, and height, and a recent record in sports" (1963:128).

Still, while stigmatization and stigma management are widespread, it is clear that the experience of stigma and the strategies used to manage it can vary widely, depending on social contexts and resources. One important contextual feature for the groups I have studied is their rich and extensive subcultures. By virtue of their longstanding subcultures, gun collectors have social and symbolic resources at their disposal that are quite different from those of more isolated deviants, such as self-injurers (Adler and Adler 2005) or bankrupt debtors (Thorne and Anderson 2006). This is particularly evident in their use of collective stigma management strategies. However, it is important to recognize that subcultures themselves may also vary significantly in their organizational contexts and resources. Some subcultures, such as those of the homeless (Snow and Anderson 1993) or the mentally ill (Estroff 1981; and Herman 1987), arise as secondary adjustments to oppressive conditions and provide relatively weak social and material support to their members. Yet others, perhaps most notably gay and lesbian subculture, are organizationally far richer and more multifaceted. As this chapter has demonstrated, subcultural organization enables the development of collective out-group and in group stigma management. Although the specific manifestations of these strategies may vary, many of the same basic types of practices are used across a wide range of social groups.

Additional comparative examinations of both out and in group stigma management techniques conducted using similar methodologies could be expected to reveal further similarities, as well as patterns of variation, across a range of deviant populations, from the intensely stigmatized to those whose members are viewed with only modest or ambivalent disapproval. The goal of such analyses, as with this paper, should be to develop a richer sociological understanding of the range of stigma management strategies and the conditions under which different patterns are likely to emerge. Continuing ethnographic examination of stigma management will only serve to complement our existing knowledge of the "deviance process" (Pfuhl 1986).

But such studies make yet another important sociological contribution. Studies such as this suggest the relevance of key concepts in the sociology of deviance for illuminating a far wider range of social relationships and interactions. As Adler and Adler have noted, deviance "has always been, and will always be, one of our most encompassing sociological tools" (2006:144). In this chapter I have supported their claim by demonstrating the value of the interactionist analysis of stigma and stigma management for illuminating previously neglected dimensions of the social worlds of gun collectors and enthusiasts.

CHAPTER VII

Discussion and Implications

Given the June 26, 2008, 5-4 decision handed down by the Supreme Court, it is clear that we, as a nation, will continue to add to the over 200,000,000 guns already in circulation. Supporting data suggest that existing guns are distributed among close to half of all U.S. households. Although their presence is not appreciated by everyone equally, their presence and impact on U.S. culture is undeniable. As I have demonstrated throughout this ethnographic account, through the telling of gun owner stories and examples of gun symbolism that permeates U.S. social institutions in the form of family influence, media exposure, history and political ideologies, we are all touched, to varying degrees, by the presence and meaning of guns.

It is clear that the presence of guns in the United States cannot be reduced to notions as simple as a second amendment right to bear arms or need to disarm the population due to safety concerns. Project data reveal that guns remain as a source of masculine social capital, a highly patriarchal and protected social arena, a source of both stigmatized and valued social capital, and a common site around which social rituals are performed. More specifically, the data reveal some interesting patterns, which are not limited to the following: 1) Guns, as an aspect of culture, or product of social interaction, are rich with multifarious symbolic values; 2) For many gun owners, the value placed on guns is far more emotional in nature than monetary; 3) The symbolic value ascribed to guns by their owners appears to influence the way in which gun owners interact with their guns as well as their social audience; 4) Gun owners recognize a unique type of stigma or suspect identity associated with these cultural products, and respond through a complex series of stigma management techniques; and 5) U.S. gun culture involves a series of deference and demeanor-filled rituals; rituals pertaining to being the gun owner, the gun user, and possibly even the gun as an object of near-worship. These ritual activities surrounding guns present rare opportunities for males to express what are often otherwise suppressed emotions – such as expressing how loved and important other influential males are to them by talking up a shared gun experience instead of addressing the loved one directly.

It is worth noting that the sensitivity to stigma among gun owners is common enough and strong enough to consider for social policy. The preliminary findings of this study suggest that gun owners would be very receptive to initiatives as simple as public service announcements and media coverage admonishing (or stigmatizing) those who use or store firearms incorrectly. As was discussed at length, safety and appropriate use are highly-important issues to gun advocacy groups. This is evidenced not only in literature common at gun shows and among various pro-gun organizations, but also through the educational and training services proactively supported by them. This is one area where there is great potential for both pro and anti-gun groups to agree on something: stigmatize the misuse of guns and you will save lives. By stigmatizing the misuse of guns (instead of gun ownership itself), policy makers and political action groups avoid the pitfalls and countless debates over issues such as treading on the liberties of others. Another advantage is that such initiatives would be relatively quick and cost-effective, as well.

Although this ethnographic account touches only on one small sample population of gun owners, collectors and enthusiasts, the data reveal that attitudes, values, meanings, beliefs and actions pertaining to guns and gun use are far more complicated than most academic treatments have surmised. Through the thick, descriptive practice of having gun owners "tell the stories of their guns," and conceptualizing guns as historical sites (with histories to be shared) while making detailed observations of how guns are situated and related to during interactions involving their use, I was able to gain a richer perspective on guns and their symbolic value than previous studies have provided.

Previous literature on the symbolic value of guns has focused narrowly on what the simple concept of gun ownership means to collectors and enthusiasts. This overlooks the possibility of intra-individual variability and that guns with different living histories and varying symbolic value might also have different outcomes (i.e. one gun might only ever be viewed as a piece of art, while the history of another ensures that it is seen only as an instrument of death). The bottom line is that it is clear that all guns are not equally likely to be used in the commission of violent acts. This will vary widely, contingent not only on culturally-specific differences such as level and nature of "pistolization" or the process through which the integration of guns into daily activity and decision making becomes a normal routine (Cukier and Sheptycki 2012), but also the specific history of the gun relative to the owner.

Existing research on gun ownership and presence, in general, has focused on the direct correlation between U.S. gun volume (availability per household) and related acts of violence and injury, directing policy attention primarily toward licensing and private ownership of guns. These existing research efforts will be informed and complemented by the present study. An understanding of the everyday, lived reality of gun-related behavior will help us to comprehend how people conceptualize their use and ownership of guns, and enhance our understanding of the probability, desirability and necessity of various gun-control measures.

The assumption that more guns equal more violence proceeds with the faulty premise that each gun is equally likely to be used to commit an act of violence. Based on my data, I suggest that every gun within a collection has the potential to hold a separate symbolic value for the owner. These symbolic values are contingent on the gun's living history; and, consequently, have the potential to influence the interaction rituals and behavior of the owners in very different ways. I argue that the living history and symbolic value ascribed to each gun has a direct influence on the outcomes associated with each gun. Additionally, as was revealed in this study, many gun collectors, who own hundreds of guns, not only commit no crimes with them, but have nothing but disdain for anyone who would "disrespect a gun" by using it in a threatening, unsafe or otherwise inappropriate manner.

Future gun-related research will only benefit from further consideration of the symbolic value imbued in individual guns, the ways in which social institutions, such as family and media inform these values, and the resulting deference and demeanor-based rituals involving the ownership and use of guns. In order to capture these data, guns must be conceptualized not only as an object capable of unleashing awful power, but also a site around which living histories are built and rituals conducted. For the purpose of this study, gun-related data were collected by following the lead taken by Hunt (2008) who emphasized the significance of capturing a "living history" by being enmeshed in the process of "serious leisure" surrounding the historical sites of interest. Instead of looking to historical sites such as battlefields, I simply treated guns as a site or place to be reconstructed and their respective stories as the history to be understood. I recommend this technique for future research projects. However, it is also possible that survey instruments could be expanded or developed to gauge a deeper level of symbolic meaning ascribed to various guns owned by research subjects – asking subject to reflect not only on what the concepts of guns and gun rights mean to them, but to list their guns and their meanings (ex. family security, right to bear arms, family history, monetary value, distrust of law enforcement/Government, etc.). In doing so, researchers will then be in a better position to ferret out relationships between specific gun-related symbolic values and gun crimes/violence.

The serious leisure pursuits studied throughout this research project involved gun owning and collecting. My fieldstudy on gun owners was conducted from January 2005 to January 2008. Field research included approximately 250 hours of direct interaction with research subjects in a variety of leisure settings, including gun shows and live action play groups (e.g., "cowboy clubs"). A total of 75 semi-structured interviews (see interview schedule in appendix A) of varying length were conducted with a range of gun collectors and other gun owners in venues that included gun collectors' homes, different kinds of shooting events, and public gun shows throughout the Midwest.

An analysis of symbolic gun representations in popular magazines and music lyrics was also conducted. My review of gun images in popular gun-related magazines supported Vigorito and Curry's (1998) and Carter and Steiner's (2003) findings that gender identity in popular magazine depictions still point to separate social expectations for men and women. Although guns as a source of symbolic empowerment was established by Jiobu and Curry (2001), and guns as a masculine power symbol by Brown (1994), gender expressions of guns in music is an unexplored area of social inquiry. My findings reveal that similar to popular magazine depictions of males and females, popular song lyrics involving guns reveal a decidedly gendered world, highly patriarchal and protective of traditional masculinity.

Although this project only analyzed two forms of popular culture, as this served the purpose of illustrating the separate treatment of men and women in multiple media outlets, additional research in this area might consider gun representations of gender in other forms of media entertainment. Gun references are by-no-means limited to song lyrics and magazines. As was reported in the first book in this series, according to the June 30, 2008 International Movie Data Base listings (http://www.imdb.com/chart/), 6 of the top ten grossing films of the week featured characters with guns (*Wanted, Get Smart, The Incredible Hulk, Indiana Jones and the Kingdom of the Crystal Skull, and You Don't Mess With the Zohan*), as did seven of the top ten DVD rentals (*Rambo, National Treasure: Book of Secrets, Mad Money, Untraceable, Grace is Gone, Cleaner and First Sunday*). Nielsen broadcast television ratings for the week of June 16, 2008 listed shows featuring characters with guns (*CSI Miami* and *CSI NY*) as being the fifth and sixth most watched, respectively (www.nielsenmedia.com). As of December 13, 2012, the trend had not changed. The top grossing box office film is the gun-heavy James Bond film *Skyfall*, followed by *Lincoln, Red Dawn and Killing Them Softly* – all with significant gun-related themes. The TV viewing trends have not reversed since 2008. If anything, more guns are prominently featured in the primetime line-ups and popular shows. The December 13, 2012, Nielsen broadcast television ratings are dominated by Cop dramas, with NCIS listed with the top viewership, and NCIS – Los Angeles and Person of Interest claiming the seventh and eighth slots, respectively. Media entertainment outlets as far stretching as Broadway shows are relevant for further consideration. Sammy Davis Jr. could once be viewed singing, dancing and punctuating his sentences with the bullets fired from a Tommy gun in the 1950s musical *Guys and Dolls*. These are untapped but important aspects of U.S. gun culture that have the potential to reveal a more detailed understanding of guns and gun use in the U.S., and deserve the attention of future research studies.

Concealed Carry Laws by State

ALABAMA
Website: http://www.ago.alabama.gov/
Page-Gun-Reprocity-Law%20
Issuing authority: County Sheriff
Cost: $1
Length: 1 year
Terms of issuance: may issue
Reciprocity: yes
Out of state permits: no
Note: Non-resident permits from other states will
be recognized, but this is subject to change.

ALASKA
Website: http://dps.state.ak.us/Statewide/
PermitsLicensing/concealed handguns.aspx
Issuing authority: Department of Public
Safety, apply at State Trooper office
Cost: $91.50 initial/$25 renewal
Length: up to 5 years
Terms of issuance: shall issue
Reciprocity: yes
Out of state permits: no
Note: while a permit is available, none is
required to carry concealed in Alaska

ARIZONA
Website: http://www.azdps.gov/ Services/

Concealed_Weapons/ Issuing authority:
Department of Public Safety, Concealed
Weapons Permits Unit
Cost: $60 initial/$43 renewal
Length: 5 years
Terms of issuance: shall issue
Reciprocity: yes
Out of state permits: yes
Note: while a permit is available, none is
required to carry concealed in Arizona

ARKANSAS
Website: http://www.asp.state.
ar.us/divisions/rs/rs_chl.html
Issuing authority: Department of State Police
Cost: $147.25 initial plus fingerprints/$63 renewal
Length: 5 years
Terms of issuance: shall issue
Reciprocity: yes
Out of state permits: no

CALIFORNIA
Website: http://oag.ca.gov/sites/all/files/
pdfs/firearms/forms/Cfl2007.pdf
Issuing authority: County Sheriff or Chief of Police
Cost: varies
Length: 2 years max
Terms of issuance: may issue
Reciprocity: no
Out of state permits: no

COLORADO
Website: http://www.denvergov.
org/CriminalInvestigationsDivision/
ConcealedWeaponsPermit/
tabid/392270/Default.aspx
Issuing authority: County Sheriff
Cost: Not to exceed $100.
Length: 5 years

Terms of issuance: shall issue
Reciprocity: yes
Out of state permits: no

CONNECTICUT
Website: http://www.ct.gov/despp/cwp/view.
asp?a=4213&q=494614&desppNav_GID=2080
Issuing authority: Chief of Police or First
Selectman, State Police for non-residents
Cost: $70
Length: 5 years
Terms of issuance: may issue
Reciprocity: no
Out of state permits: yes
Note: must apply for a local permit
prior to eligibility for State permit

DELAWARE
Website: http://courts.delaware.
gov/Superior/weapons.stm
Issuing authority: Prothonotary of Superior Court
Cost: $65.00 initial/renewal
Length: 2 years initial/3 renewal
Terms of issuance: may issue
Reciprocity: yes
Out of state permits: no
Note: statute allows 3-year initial permit/5
renewal, but procedural rules only allow 2/3

FLORIDA
Website: http://licgweb.doacs.state.
fl.us/weapons/index.html
Issuing authority: Dep't of Agriculture and
Consumer Services, Division of Licensing
Cost: $112 initial, $60-102 renewal
Length: 7 years
Terms of issuance: shall issue
Reciprocity: yes
Out of state permits: yes

GEORGIA
Website: http://dps.georgia.gov/georgias-firearm-
permit-reciprocity (reciprocity information only)
Issuing authority: County Probate Judge
Cost: $30 plus additional fees that vary by county
Length: 5 years
Terms of issuance: shall issue
Reciprocity: yes
Out of state permits: no

HAWAII
Website: http://honolulupd.org/info/gunlaw.htm
Issuing authority: Chief of Police
Cost: $10
Length: 1 year
Terms of issuance: may issue
"in an exceptional case"
Reciprocity: no
Out of state permits: unlikely
Note: permits are limited to
carrying in the counties in which they are
issued. While out-of-state permits are not
specifically provided for, the statute authorizes
permits for selective foreign nationals

IDAHO
Website: http://www.ag.idaho.gov/
concealedWeapons/concealedWeaponsjndex.html
Issuing authority: County Sheriff
Cost: $20 initial plus additional fees/$15 renewal
Length: 5 years
Terms of issuance: shall issue
Reciprocity: yes
Out of state permits: yes

ILLINOIS
Website: http://www.isp.state.
il.us/foid/firearmsfaq.cfm
Issuing authority: None

Cost: n/a
Length: n/a
Terms of issuance: n/a
Reciprocity: n/a
Out of state permits: n/a
Note: concealed carry is not allowed in Illinois

INDIANA
Website: http://www.in.gov/isp/2828.htm
Issuing authority: State Police through
local chief law enforcement officer
Cost: $10-50.
Length: 4 years or lifetime
Terms of issuance: shall issue
Reciprocity: yes
Out of state permits: yes
Note: out of state permits appear to only be issued
to those with a regular place of business in Indiana

IOWA
Website: http://www.dps.state.ia.us/regassist/
FAQ_fact_sheets/SF2379_FAQ.pdf
Issuing authority: County Sheriff
Cost: $50 initial/$25 renewal
Length: 5-year nonprofessional, 1 year professional
Terms of issuance: shall issue
Reciprocity: yes
Out of state permits: yes, professional only
Note: contact Commissioner of Public Safety for out of state permit

KANSAS
Website: http://ag.ks.gov/public-
safety/concealedcarry
Issuing authority: Attorney General
through County Sheriff
Cost: $132.50 initial/$25 renewal
Length: 4 years
Terms of issuance: shall issue
Reciprocity: yes

Out of state permits: no

KENTUCKY
Website: http://www.kentuckystatepolice.
org/conceal.htm
Issuing authority: State Police
through County Sheriff
Cost: $60 initial/$60 renewal
Length: 5 years
Terms of issuance: shall issue
Reciprocity: yes
Out of state permits: no

LOUISIANA
Website: http://www.lsp.org/handguns.html
Issuing authority: Department of
Public Safety and Corrections
Cost: $125 initial/renewal, $62.50
initial/renewal if 65 or over
Length: 5 years
Terms of issuance: shall issue
Reciprocity: yes
Out of state permits: no

MAINE
Website: http://www.maine.gov/dps/
msp/licenses/weapons_permits.html
Issuing authority: varies by area of residence:
Mayor/municipal authority or Chief of State Police
Cost: $35 intial/$20 renewal ($60 for non-residents)
Length: 4 years
Terms of issuance: shall issue
Reciprocity: yes
Out of state permits: yes
Note: reciprocity applies only to resident permits

MARYLAND
Website: http://www.mdsp.org/ Organization/SupportServicesBureau/
LicensingDivision/HandgunPermit.aspx

Issuing authority: State Police
Cost: $109.50 initial/$66.50 renewal
Length: 2 years initial/3 years renewal
Terms of issuance: statute reads "shall issue," but requires a showing of need
Reciprocity: no
Out of state permits: yes

MASSACHUSETTS
Website: http://www.mass.gov/ eopss/firearms-reg-and-laws/
Issuing authority: Colonel of State Police/Firearms Record Bureau
Cost: $100
Length: 5-6 years
Terms of issuance: may issue
Reciprocity: no
Out of state permits: yes

MICHIGAN
Website: http://www.michigan.gov/ ag/0,4534,7-164-58056^22672—.OO.html
Issuing authority: County Concealed Weapon Licensing Board
Cost: $105 initial and renewal
Length: 5 years
Terms of issuance: shall issue
Reciprocity: yes
Out of state permits: no
Note: reciprocity not extended to non-resident permits

MINNESOTA
Website: https://www.revisor.mn.gov/ statutes/?id=624.714&year=2011
Issuing authority: County Sheriff
Cost: $100 or less initial/$75 or less renewal
Length: 5 years
Terms of issuance: shall issue
Reciprocity: yes

Out of state permits: yes

MISSISSIPPI
Website: http://www.dps.state.ms.us/
firearms/firearms-perm it-unit/
Issuing authority: Department of Public Safety
Cost: $132 initial/$82 renewal
Length: 5 years
Terms of issuance: shall issue
Reciprocity: yes
Out of state permits: no

MISSOURI
Website: http://ago.mo.gov/Concealed-Weapons/
Issuing authority: County or City Sheriff
Cost: $100 or less initial/$50 or less renewal
Length: 3 years
Terms of issuance: shall issue
Reciprocity: yes
Out of state permits: no

MONTANA
Website: http://doj.mt.gov/enforcement/
concealed-weapons/
Issuing authority: County Sheriff
Cost: $50 initial/$25 renewal
Length: 4 years
Terms of issuance: shall issue
Reciprocity: yes
Out of state permits: no

NEBRASKA
Website: http://statepatrol.nebraska.
gov/Concealed_FAQ.aspx
Issuing authority: State Patrol
Cost: $100 initial/$50 renewal
Length: 5 years
Terms of issuance: shall issue
Reciprocity: yes

Out of state permits: no

NEVADA
Website: http://www.lvmpd.com/ Permits/ConcealedFirearms.aspx
Issuing authority: County Sheriff
Cost: $60 initial/$25 renewal, plus additional fees.
Length: 5 years
Terms of issuance: shall issue
Reciprocity: yes
Out of state permits: yes

NEW HAMPSHIRE
Website: http://www.nh.gov/safety/divisions/
nhsp/ssb/permitslicensing/plupr.html
Issuing authority: Selectman/Mayor or Chief of Police, State Police for
non-residents
Cost: $10 resident/$100 non-resident
Length: 4 years
Terms of issuance: shall issue
Reciprocity: yes
Out of state permits: yes
Note: reciprocity not extended
to non-resident permits

NEW JERSEY
Website: http://www.state.nj.us/
njsp/about/fi re_ag2.html
Issuing authority: Chief of Police/
Superintendent of State Police/Superior Court
Cost: $20
Length: 2 years
Terms of issuance: may issue
Reciprocity: no
Out of state permits: yes

NEW MEXICO
Website: http://www.dps.nm.org/
index.php/nm-concealed-carry/
Issuing authority: Department of Public Safety

Cost: not more than $100, plus
fingerprint fee initial/$75 renewal
Length: 4 years, with requalification
required at 2 years.
Terms of issuance: shall issue
Reciprocity: yes
Out of state permits: no

NEW YORK
Website: http://www.troopers.ny.gov/Firearms/
Issuing authority: varies
Cost: not specified
Length: not specified
Terms of issuance: may issue
Reciprocity: yes
Out of state permits: no

NORTH CAROLINA
Website: http://www.ncdoj.gov/
about-doj/law-enforcement-training-
and-standards/law-enforcement-liason/
concealed-weapon-reciprocity.aspx
Issuing authority: County Sheriff
Cost: $80 plus fingerprints initial/$75 renewal
Length: 5 years
Terms of issuance: shall issue
Reciprocity: yes
Out of state permits: no

NORTH DAKOTA
Website: http://www.ag.nd.gov/BCI/CW/CW.htm
Issuing authority: Bureau of Criminal Investigation
through local Sheriff/Chief of Police
Cost: $45 plus fingerprints initial/$45 renewal
Length: 5 years
Terms of issuance: shall issue
Reciprocity: yes
Out of state permits: yes

OHIO
Website: http://www.ohioattorneygeneral.
gov/ConcealedCarry.aspx/?from=nav
Issuing authority: County Sheriff
Cost: $67 initial plus other possible fees/$50
renewal plus other possible fees
Length: 5 years
Terms of issuance: shall issue
Reciprocity: yes
Out of state permits: no

OKLAHOMA
Website: http://www.ok.gov/osbi/
Concealed J/Veapons_Licensing/
Issuing authority: State Bureau of Investigation
Cost: $100 initial for 5 years/$85 renewal;
$200 initial for 10 years/$170 renewal
Length: 5 years or 10 years
Terms of issuance: shall issue
Reciprocity: yes
Out of state permits: no

OREGON
Website: http://licenseinfo.oregon.gov/index.
cfm?fuseaction=license_seng&link_item_id=14705
Issuing authority: County Sheriff
Cost: $65 for initial/$50 renewal
Length: 4 years
Terms of issuance: shall issue
Reciprocity: no
Out of state permits: yes

PENNSYLVANIA
Website: http://www.portal.state.pa.us/
portal/server.pt?open=512&objlD=4451&&P
agelD=462424&level=2&css=L2&mode=2
Issuing authority: County Sheriff/Chief of Police
Cost: $25
Length: 5 years

Terms of issuance: shall issue
Reciprocity: yes
Out of state permits: yes

RHODE ISLAND
Website: http://www.riag.ri.gov/
documents/bci/pistols.pdf
Issuing authority: Attorney General
Cost: $40
Length: 4 years
Terms of issuance: may issue
Reciprocity: no (limited reciprocity extended to
those passing through the state without delay)
Out of state permits: yes
Note: under 11-47-18 the Attorney General may issue a
permit based on a showing of need, but
11 -47-11 provides that local licensing authorities
shall issue a permit to a qualified applicant

SOUTH CAROLINA
Website: http://www.sled.sc.gov/
cwp.aspx?MenulD=CWP
Issuing authority: S.C. Law Enforcement Division
Cost: $50 initial or renewal
Length: 4 years
Terms of issuance: shall issue
Reciprocity: yes
Out of state permits: only if applicant
owns real estate property in S.C.

SOUTH DAKOTA
Website: http://sdsos.gov/content/
viewcontent.aspx?cat=adminservices&pg=/
adminservices/concealedpistolpermits.shtm
Issuing authority: Secretary of
State through County Sheriff
Cost: $10
Length: 4 years
Terms of issuance: shall issue

Reciprocity: yes
Out of state permits: no

TENNESSEE
Website: http://www.tn.gov/
safety/handgunmain.shtml
Issuing authority: Tennessee Department
of Safety/Highway Patrol
Cost: $115 initial/$50 renewal
Length: 4 years
Terms of issuance: shall issue
Reciprocity: yes
Out of state permits: yes
Note: out of state permits currently
only provided to those who are
regularly employed in the state

TEXAS
Website: http://www.txdps.state.tx.us/
administration/crime_records/chl/chlsindex.htm
Issuing authority: Department of Public Safety
Cost: $140 initial/$70 renewal
Length: 4 years initial, 5 for renewal
Terms of issuance: shall issue
Reciprocity: yes
Out of state permits: yes

UTAH
Website: http://www.publicsafety.utah.
gov/bci/concealedfi rearms.html
Issuing authority: Department of Public
Safety, Bureau of Criminal Identification
Cost: $46 initial ($51 for out of
state)/$15 renewal (all)
Length: 5 years
Terms of issuance: shall issue
Reciprocity: yes
Out of state permits: yes
Note: Currently out of state permits only issued

to non-residents from states granting
concealed carry.

VERMONT
Website: http://www.atg.state.
vt. us/issues/gun-laws. php
Issuing authority: no permit required
Cost: n/a
Length: n/a
Terms of issuance: n/a
Reciprocity: n/a
Out of state permits: n/a
Note: no permit required for concealed carry

VIRGINIA
Website: http://www.vsp.state.va.us/Firearms.shtm
Issuing authority: Circuit Court
Cost: $50 or less
Length: 5 years
Terms of issuance: shall issue
Reciprocity: yes
Out of state permits: yes

WASHINGTON
Website: http://www.atg.wa.gov/
ConcealedWeapons.aspx
Issuing authority: Chief of Police/Sheriff
Cost: $36. Initial with additional fees/$32 renewal
Length: 5 years
Terms of issuance: shall issue
Reciprocity: yes
Out of state permits: yes

WEST VIRGINIA
Website: http://www.wvago.gov/gunrecep.cfm
Issuing authority: County Sheriff
Cost: $75 plus $15 in fees
Length: 5 years
Terms of issuance: shall issue

Reciprocity: yes
Out of state permits: no

WISCONSIN
Website: http://www.doj.state.wi.us/
dles/cib/ConcealedCarry/ccw_
frequently_askedjquestions.pdf
Issuing authority: Department of Justice
Cost: less than $37 plus cost of background
check initial (max of $50)/ less than $12
plus cost of background check renewal
Length: 5 years
Terms of issuance: shall issue
Reciprocity: yes
Out of state permits: no

WYOMING
Website: http://attorneygeneral.state.wy.us/dci/
Issuing authority: Attorney General
though County Sheriff
Cost: $74 for initial plus possible
other fees/$50 renewal
Length: 5 years
Terms of issuance: shall issue
Reciprocity: yes
Out of state permits: no

Semi-Structured Interview Questions

Ohio State University IRB Exemption 2007E0255
Interview Questions: U.S. Gun Culture

1. Do you own a gun (y/n)?
   (if the answer is no, skip to question 8)
2. At what approximate age did you receive your first gun?
3. Was it a gift, or did you purchase it?
4. If your first gun was a gift, who gave it to you?
5. If you purchased your first gun for yourself, what made you decide to purchase it?
6. Do you subscribe to any gun-related publications (ex. Magazines), y/n? _____ If the answer is yes, to which gun-related publications do you subscribe (if no, skip to question 8)?

   _____

7. Do gun-related publications influence your decisions related to gun purchases? _____ If you answered yes, how so?

   _____

8. Was your first gun a pistol, rifle, shotgun, or other (if other, please describe)?
9. How many guns do you currently own? Pistols_____, Rifles_____, Shotguns_____, others (please list)

   _____

10. Do others within your household own guns (y/n)? _____ If the answer is yes, approximately how many additional guns, other than those in your own collection are in your household (y/n)? ____ Please tell me about them. What other guns are in your household (please fill in the approximate quantity)? Pistols_____, Rifles_____, Shotguns_____, others (please list)

_____

11. Have you ever attended another gun show or gun event (y/n)? _____ (If yes, approximately how many? _____ If no, skip to question 11)

12. Please fill in the approximate number of times you have attended the following types of gun-related events: gun clubs _____, shooting tournaments _____, live action role play events _____, other (please describe)

_____

13. What is your age?
14. What is your state of birth?
15. In which U.S. state do you currently reside?
16. Which best describes the community in which you were raised (circle all that apply)? Rural, urban, suburb, or mid-size town (population between 25,000 – 50,000)
17. Which best describes the community in which you currently live (circle 1)? Rural, urban, suburb, or mid-size town (population between 25,000 – 50,000)
18. What is your highest level of education completed (circle one)? High School, Junior/Community College Certificate or Associates Degree, Four Year Degree, Graduate/professional School?
19. Do you use a gun as part of your profession/job?
20. Do you have a favorite gun?_____ (If yes, why is it your favorite? If no, skip to question 20)

_____
_____
_____
_____

21. Does your favorite gun have a name? _____ (If yes, what did you name it? _____)

22. How/why did you pick this particular name?

    _____

23. What would you say guns mean to you?

24. If you have stories related to any of your guns (ex. First hunting or shooting experience, or something special about one or more of your guns), please share your story or stories with me. Try to be as specific about the style, type and model of gun as possible. Use extra space if necessary.

25. Please list your guns in the order that you received or purchased them (that is, arrange them in order by how long they have been in your possession, from longest time in your collection to most recent acquisition). Please provide the caliber and brand/model of each if known. Next, indicate which of your guns your consider to be the most valuable, and why? (Please be sure to state if the value that you place on the gun is based on actual/monetary value, or more personal/sentimental reasons).

Consent Form

The Ohio State University Consent to Participate in Research

Study Title:	Gun Shows, Gun Collectors and the Story of the Gun: An Ethnographic Approach to U.S. Gun Culture
Researcher:	Jim Taylor and Timothy J. Curry
Sponsor:	

This is a consent form for research participation. It contains important information about this study and what to expect if you decide to participate.

Your participation is voluntary.

Please consider the information carefully. Feel free to ask questions before making your decision whether or not to participate. If you decide to participate, you will be asked to sign this form and will receive a copy of the form.

Purpose:

You are being asked to participate in this study on U.S. gun culture. The purpose of this study is to collect the individual stories of gun collectors, gun enthusiasts, and second amendment advocates, in order to gain a better understanding of U.S. gun culture, gun-related traditions, and the values that individuals assign to guns. Guns have had a unique presence in U.S. history, and relatively little is known about the culture and deep social meaning associated with guns and gun ownership. The more that is known about guns and gun owners, the better understanding we will have of ourselves as a common people.

Procedures/Tasks:

Participants will be interviewed about their guns or gun-related activities on a strictly voluntary basis and asked to fill out a brief questionnaire. In addition to filling out a questionnaire, gun owners will be asked to set up a time to share stories about their guns, how they came to be gun owners, and what their guns mean to them. Additionally, owners of gun collections or rare firearms will be asked for permission to photograph their guns, in order to illustrate the symbols, craftsmanship, artwork and general detail that will be described by the gun owners. Gun owners will not be filmed or photographed, only the guns and gun displays. Interviews will be audio taped. The tapes will be kept in a locked filing cabinet in the researchers office, and no one else will have access to the locked cabinet. Tapes will be kept until the information is transcribed, and then erased. If photographs are taken of individual gun collections and displays, there is a possibility that they will be used in published journal articles, books, or other scholarly publications. All photographs will be saved in a password-protected database in the researcher's office. No one else will have access to the photos.

Duration:

It will take approximately 20 minutes to complete the initial questionnaire. It is estimated that each interview session with a participant will last no longer than two hours. It is estimated that each participant will be interviewed no more than three times. Basically, the length of each interview session will be determined by the participant and not by the researcher. Great attention and care will be given to the participant's comfort level, age and ability to continue discussion on the topic

You may leave the study at any time. If you decide to stop participating in the study, there will be no penalty to you, and you will not lose any benefits to which you are otherwise entitled. Your decision will not affect your future relationship with The Ohio State University.

Risks and Benefits:

No risks are anticipated, and there will be no direct benefit to individual participants. However, generally it is anticipated that this research will add to the general body of knowledge about gun culture in the U.S. Presently, very little is known about gun culture in the U.S. By learning more about how guns are thought about in the U.S. as symbols and as cultural artifacts the researchers hope to gain a better understanding of traditions and customs associated with guns and gun use.

Confidentiality:

Your name and other identifying information will not be published with the research findings.

Incentives:

You will not be paid to participate in the study

Participant Rights:

You may refuse to participate in this study without penalty or loss of benefits to which you are otherwise entitled. If you are a student or employee at Ohio State, your decision will not affect your grades or employment status.

If you choose to participate in the study, you may discontinue participation at any time without penalty or loss of benefits. By signing this form, you do not give up any personal legal rights you may have as a participant in this study.

An Institutional Review Board responsible for human subjects research at The Ohio State University reviewed this research project and found it to be acceptable, according to applicable state and federal regulations and University policies designed to protect the rights and welfare of participants in research.

Contacts and Questions:

For questions, concerns, or complaints about the study you may contact Jim Taylor at taylorj2@ohio.edu, or Professor Timothy J. Curry at 614-292-7560.

For questions about your rights as a participant in this study or to discuss other study-related concerns or complaints with someone who is not part of the research team, you may contact Ms. Sandra Meadows in the Office of Responsible Research Practices at 1-800-678-6251.

Signing the consent form

I have read (or someone has read to me) this form and I am aware that I am being asked to participate in a research study. I have had the opportunity to ask questions and have had them answered to my satisfaction. I voluntarily agree to participate in this study.

I am not giving up any legal rights by signing this form. I will be given a copy of this form.

Printed Name of Subject   Signature

_____   _____

Date and Time _____

Printed name of person   Signature of person
authorized to consent for   authorized to consent for
subject (when applicable)   subject (when applicable)

_____   _____

Relationship to subject   Date and Time _____

_____

Investigator/Research Staff

I have explained the research to the participant or his/her representative before requesting the signature(s) above. There are no blanks in this document. A copy of this form has been given to the participant or his/her representative.

Printed name of person   Signature
obtaining consent

_____   _____

Date and Time _____

Glossary of Gun Terms

Common Terms Associated with Firearms

TYPES

<u>Handgun</u> - A weapon designed to fire a small projectile from one or more barrels when held in one hand with a short stock designed to be gripped by one hand.

<u>Revolver</u> - A handgun that contains its ammunition in a revolving cylinder that typically holds five to nine cartridges, each within a separate chamber. Before a revolver fires, the cylinder rotates, and the next chamber is aligned with the barrel.

<u>Pistol</u> - Any handgun that does not contain its ammunition in a revolving cylinder. Pistols can be manually operated or semiautomatic. A semiautomatic pistol generally contains cartridges in a magazine located in the grip of the gun. When the semiautomatic pistol is fired, the spent cartridge that contained the bullet and propellant is ejected, the firing mechanism is cocked, and a new cartridge is chambered.

<u>Derringer</u> - A small single- or multiple-shot handgun other than a revolver or semiautomatic pistol.

<u>Rifle</u> - A weapon intended to be fired from the shoulder that uses the energy of the explosive in a fixed metallic cartridge to fire only a single projectile through a rifled bore for each single pull of the trigger.

Shotgun - A weapon intended to be fired from the shoulder that uses the energy of the explosive in a fixed shotgun shell to fire through a smooth bore either a number of ball shot or a single projectile for each single pull of the trigger.

FIRING ACTION

Fully automatic - Capability to fire a succession of cartridges so long as the trigger is depressed or until the ammunition supply is exhausted. Automatic weapons are considered machineguns subject to the provisions of the National Firearms Act.

Semiautomatic - An auto-loading action that will fire only a single shot for each single function of a trigger

.

Machinegun - Any weapon that shoots, is designed to shoot, or can be readily restored to shoot automatically more than one shot without manual reloading by a single function of the trigger.

Submachinegun - A simple fully automatic weapon that fires a pistol cartridge that is also referred to as a machine pistol.

AMMUNITION

Caliber - The size of the ammunition that a weapon is designed to shoot, as measured by the bullet's approximate diameter in inches in the United States and in millimeters in other countries. In some instances, ammunition is described with additional terms, such as the year of its introduction (.30/06) or the name of the designer (.30 Newton). In some countries, ammunition is also described in terms of the length of the cartridge case (7.62 x 63 mm).

Gauge - For shotguns, the number of spherical balls of pure lead, each exactly fitting the bore, that equals one pound.

Firearms Terms. Adapted from Bureau of Justice Statistics July, 1995 report "Guns Used in Crime and ATF, Firearms S Explosives Tracing Guidebook, September 1993, pp. 35-40, May-June 1991, pp. 195-215. Retrieved November 10, 2007 from http://www.ojp.usdoj.gov/bjs/pub/pdf/guic.pdf.

Common Gun-Related Sayings

Aim higher/lower - Setting goals.

Blow your load - A male's ejaculation.

Bite the bullet - to do the right thing even if the result will not work out in your favor.

Bullet Proof - To be or believe to be invincible.

a Burner - Also known as a hand gun.

Copper - An AK-47 assault rifle.

Drop the hammer - To crack down on something.

Easier than shooting fish in a barrel - Something that is very simple.

Faster than a speeding bullet - Used to explain how fast something was going if it seemed to go at a high rate of speed.

Gatt - A gun.

Get the lead out – A request to pick up the pace or move faster.

Going off half-cocked - Getting mad about something and not having all of the relevant information or details.

Gun – To rev an engine excessively or floor the excelerator.

Gun Shy - Cautious.

Hotter than a pistol - An expression used to express how mad someone is.

Hotter than a two dollar pistol – Something that is believed to be stolen.

In my sights – Something or someone clearly visible and in range.

In your cross hairs - Something or someone in your immediate path.

Jump the gun – To act prematurely, or alternately, to start a race before the starting gun sounds.

Just shoot me now - An expression used to signify that a person is in a difficult situation and would rather not deal with the unpleasant aftermath.

Loaded - The altered state of a person under the influence of controlled substances.

Lock, stock, and barrel - All, total,everything.

Lock and load – Ready to go.

Loose Cannon - Cannot be predicted.

No one held a gun to your head – An expression used to signify that no relevant party was forced into something.

Overshot - Something landed past target or alternately, someone was way off base in an estimate or platitude.

Pull the trigger - To take decisive action with no certainty of the outcome.

Rapid Fire - Quickly or one after another in rapid succession.

She let me have it with both barrels - Meant to signify big trouble with a spouse or significant other.

Shelling out - Paying for something.

Shot in the dark - Taking a guess.

Shot glass - A glass that only holds an ounce of liquor.

Shooting blind - When someone has no idea what they are doing.

Shoot - Commonly used in place of the swear word shit.

Shot down - To be told no without consideration.

Shot Gun Wedding - A wedding that happens very quickly and possibly under extreme duress.

Shot to hell - When plans fall through.

Shoot first, ask questions later - To act decisively, without hesitation.

Shoot from the hip - To be brutally honest.

Shot myself in the foo t- To unintentionally undermine one's self.

Shoot out - To fiercely compete in an activity until someone wins.

Shoot the Breeze -Telling tall tales and casual stories.

Show your guns - To flex mussels.

Smoking gun - Evidence in a case that will make the whole case for a side.

Stick to your guns – Stay the course.

Straight Shooter - A person that is right to the point when they are talking.

Taking aim - Setting a goal.

Taking out the big guns - To bring out the best evidence of excellence, achievement, or proof of dominance.

That girl is bangin' - Contemporary urban expression used to signify that a woman is a worthy objective of sexual desire.

Under the gun – Under pressure.

Worth a shot - Worth the chance.

With guns blazing - Hell bent. With excessively determined purpose. Damn the consequences.

Gun Culture in the United States Approach Script

Hello, my name is Jim Taylor. I am a researcher and instructor in the Sociology Department at Ohio State University. I am conducting research, speaking with gun collectors and gun enthusiasts about their stories and thoughts on guns. Primarily, I am interested in seeing gun collections, photographing them, and in audio-taping gun collectors as they tell stories about their guns and gun-related experiences. It is anticipated that no interview session will run longer than two hours, and the collector can name the location, date, and time of the interview.

Would you be willing to talk with me or do you know of someone I could contact who might be interested in talking to me?

Me Out In The Field With "The Last Cowboy"

Photo by Katherine A. Taylor

References

Adler, Patricia A. and Peter Adler. 1987. *Membership Roles in Field Research.*Newbury Park, CA: Sage.

_____. 2005. "Self-Injurers as Loners: The Social Organization of Solitary Deviance." *Deviant Behavior* 26:345-378.

_____. 2006. "The Deviance Society." *Deviant Behavior* 27:129-148.

Anderson, Leon. 2006. "Analytic Autoethnography." *Journal of Contemporary Ethnography* 35: 373-395.

Anderson, Leon, and Thomas C. Calhoun. 1992. "Facilitative Aspects of Field Research with Deviant Street Populations." *Sociological Inquiry* 62:490-498.

Birrell, Susan. 1981. "Sport as Ritual: Interpretations from Durkheim and Goffman." *Social Forces.* 60(2):354-376.

Berger, Peter; and Thomas Luckmann. 1966. *The Social Construction of Reality: A Treatise in the Sociology of Knowledge.* Garden City, NY: Doubleday.

Brady Campaign to Prevent Gun Violence. "The Six Federal Gun Laws." Accessed on April 16, 2008, at http://www.bradycampaign.org/legislation/federal/pages.php?page=6fedla ws

Browder, Laura. 2006. *Her Best Shot: Women and Guns in America.* Chapel Hill, NC: The University of North Carolina Press.

Brown, Ian. 1994. *Man Medium Rare: Sex, Guns and Other Perversions of Masculinity.* New York: Dutton.

Carter, Cynthia and Linda Steiner. 2003.*Critical Readings: Media and Gender Issues in Cultural and Media Studies.* London: Open University Press.

Charmaz, Kathy. 2006. *Constructing Grounded Theory: A Practical Guide Through Qualitative Analysis.* Thousand Oaks, CA: Sage.

Collins, Randall. 2004. Interaction Ritual Chains. Princeton, NJ: Princeton University Press

Connell, R.W. 2005. *Masculinities* (2nd ed.). Los Angeles, CA: University of California Press.

_____.2000. *The Men and the Boys*. Los Angeles, CA: University of California Press.

_____. 1987. *Gender and Power: Society, the Person, and Sexual Politics*. Stanford, CA: Stanford University Press.

Courtenay, W.H. 2000. "Construction of Masculinities and Their Influence on Men's Well-Being: A Theory of Gender and Health." *Social Science & Medicine*. 50:1385-1401.

Cox, Amy Ann. 2007. "Aiming for Manhood: The Transformation of Guns Into Objects of American Masculinity." Pp. 141-149 in *Open Fire: Understanding Global Gun Cultures*, edited by Charles Fruehling Springwood. Oxford, UK: Berg Publishers..

Cramer, Clayton. 1999. *Concealed Weapon Laws of the Early Republic*. Westport, CT: Praeger Publishing.

Cromwell, Paul, and Quint Thurman. 2003. "The Devil Made Me Do It: Use of Neutralizations by Shoplifters." *Deviant Behavior* 24:535-550.

Cukier, Wendy. 2012. "Globalization of Gun Culture Transnational Reflections on Pistolization and Masculinity, Flows and Resistance." *International Journal of Law, Crime and Justice* 40:3-19.

Darling-Wolf, Fabienne. 2004. "SMAP, Sex and Masculinity: Constructing the Perfect Female Fantasy in Japanese Popular Music." *Popular Music and Society* 27(3):357-370.

Davidoff, Leonore. 1990. "Adam Spoke First and Named the Orders of the World: Masculine and Feminine Domains in History and Sociology." Pp. 229-255 in *Politics of Everyday Life*, edited by Helen Corr and Lynn Jamison. London: Macmillan.

Durkheim, Emile. 1965/1912. *Elementary Forms of the Religious Life*. CA: The Free Press.

Estroff, Sue E. 1981. *Making It Crazy: An Ethnography of Psychiatric Clients in an American Community*. Berkeley: University of California Press.

Evans, Tony and Patti Wallace. 2008. "A Prison Within a Prison? The Masculinity Narratives of Male Prisoners." *Men and Masculinities*. 10(4):484-507.

Ferrell, Jeff and Mark S. Hamm. 1998. *Ethnography at the Edge: Crime, Deviance and Field Research*. Boston, MA: Northeastern University Press.

Flugel, Ingeborg. 1931. "Some Psychological Aspects of a Fox-Hunting Rite." *The Journal of International Psycho-Analysis*. 12:483-491.

Geertz, Clifford R. 1973. *The Interpretation of Cultures.* Harper.

Glaser, Barney. 2001. *The Grounded Theory Perspective: Conceptualization Contrasted with Description.* Mill Valley, CA: The Sociology Press.

Glaser, Barney and Anslem Strauss. 1967. *The Discovery of Grounded Theory: Strategies for Qualitative Research.* New York: Aldine Publishing.

Goffman, Erving. 1963. *Stigma: Notes on the Management of Spoiled Identity.* New York: Simon and Schuster.

_____. 1967. *Interaction Ritual: Essays on Face to Face Behavior.* New York: Pantheon.

_____. 1979. *Gender in Advertisements.* Boston, MA: Harvard Press.

Gottlieb, Joanne and Gayle Wald. 1994. "Smells Like Teen Spirit: Riot Grrrls, Revolution and Women in Independent Rock." PP 260-274 in *Microphone Friends: Youth Music & Youth Culture,* edited by Andrew Ross and Tricia Ross. New York: Routledge.

Grossman, David, Beth Mueller, Christine Riedy, Denise Dowd, Andres Villaveces, Janice Prodzinski, Jon Nakagawara, John Howard, Norman Thiersch and Richard Harruff. 2005. Gun Storage Practices and Risk of Youth Suicides and Unintentional Firearm Injuries. 293:704-714

Herman, Nancy J. 1987. "The 'Mixed Nutters' and 'Looney Tuners': The Emergence, Development, Nature, and Functions of Two Informal, Deviant Subcultures of Chronic Ex-Psychiatric Patients." *Deviant Behavior* 8: 232-258.

_____. 1993. "Return to Sender: Reintegrative Stigma-management Strategies of Ex-Psychiatric Patients." *Journal of Contemporary Ethnography* 22:295-330.

Hewitt, John P., and Randall Stokes. 1975. "Disclaimers." *American Sociological Review* 40:1-11.

Hollander, Edwin P. 1958. "Conformity, Status, and Idiosyncrasy Credit."*Psychological Review* 65:117-127.

Hughes, Everett C. 1945. "Dilemmas and Contradictions of Status." *American Journal of Sociology* 50:353-359.

Hunt, Stephen. 2008. "But We're Real Men Aren't We! Living History as a Site of Masculine Identity Construction." *Men and Masculinities.* 10(4):460-483.

Huntington, Roy. 1997. "Fill Yer Hand, Pilgrim: Cowboy Action Shooting Sport." *Shooting Industry Magazine.* December 1997.

Hutchings, Kimberly. 2008. "Making Sense of Masculinity and War." *Men and Masculinities.* 10(4):389-404.

International Movie Database Listing. Accessed on June 30, 2008 at http://www.imdb.com/chart/.

Jiobu, Robert and Timothy J. Curry. 2001. "Lack of Confidence in the Federal Government and the Ownership of Firearms." *Social Science Quarterly.* 82:77-88.

Jordan, Ellen and Angela Cowan. 2007. 7th ed. "Warrior Narratives in the Kindergarten Classroom: Renegotiating the Social Contract?" PP. 81-93 in *Men's Lives*, edited by Michael Kimmel and Michael Messner. New York: Allyn & Bacon

Katz, Jack. 2007. "Ways of the Badass." PP. 549-574 in *Men's Lives (7th ed.)*, edited by Michael Kimmel and Michael Messner. New York: Allyn & Bacon.

Kimmel, Michael. 2000. *The Gendered Society*. New York: Oxford University Press.

Kimmel, Michael and Michael Messner. 2007. *Men's Lives* (7th ed.). New York: Allyn & Bacon.

Kirchler, Erich. 1992. "Adorable Woman, Expert Man: Changing Gender Images of Women and Men in Management." European Journal of Social Psychology. 22(4):363-373.

Kleck, Gary. 1991. *Point Blank: Guns and Violence in America*. New York: Aldine De Gruyter.

Korwin, Alan. 1995. *Gun Laws of America*. Phoenix, AZ: Bloomfield Press.

Korwin, Alan and David Kopel. 2008. The Heller Case: Gun Rights Affirmed.

Lee, Jennifer. 2005. "The Man Date." *The New York Times*. April 10.

Leonard, Marion. 2007. *Gender in the Music Industry: Rock, Discourse and Girl Power*. Burlington, VT: Achgate Publishing Company

Liggins, Marty. 2008. "Celebrities Shoot for a Cause in Nashville." Accessed on April 16, 2008, at http://www.womenandguns.com/archive/old0901issue/nashville0901.html

Lofland, John, David A. Snow, Leon Anderson, and Lyn Lofland. 2005. *Analyzing Social Settings*. Fourth ed. Belmont, CA: Thomson/Wadsworth.

Lott, John. 1998. *More Guns, Less Crime: Understanding Crime and Gun Control Laws*. Chicago: University of Chicago Press

Lyng, Stephen. 1990. "Edgework: A Social Psychological Analysis of Voluntary Risk Taking, *American Journal of Sociology* 95:851-886.

Majors, Richard and Janet Billson. 1992. *Cool Pose Expression and Survival*. Skywood Press.

Martin, Susan and Nancy Jurik. 1996. *Doing Gender, Doing Justice*. Thousand Oaks, CA: Sage Press.

Mauss, Iris, Catherine Evers, Frank Wilhelm and James Gross. 2006. "How to Bite Your Tongue Without blowing Your Top: Implicit Evaluation of Emotion Regulation Predicts Affective Responding to Anger Provocation." *Personality and Social Psychology Bulletin.* 32(5):589-602.

Mayer, Scott E. 2000. "Passing the Torch." *American Rifleman*, May, pp.34.

Messner, James. 2002. *Taking the Field: Women, Men and Sport.* Minneapolis: University of Minneapolis Press.

Messerschmidt, James W. 1997. *Crime as Structured Action.* London: Sage
_____. 2000. "Becoming "Real Men": Adolescent Masculinity Challenges and Sexual Violence." Men and Masculinities 2(3): 286-307.

Mills, C. Wright. 1940. "Situated Actions and Vocabularies of Motive." American Sociological Review 5:904-913.

National Rifle Association. 2008. "Eddie Eagle FAQs." Accessed on April 14, 2008 at http://www.nrahq.org/safety/eddie/fact.asp#01.

Nielson Broadcast Television Ratings. Accessed on June 16, 2008 at www.nielsenmedia.com.

Newton, George and Franklin Zimring. 1969. *Firearms and Violence in American Life: A Staff Report Submitted to the National Commission on the Causes and Prevention of Violence.* Washington, D.C.: U.S. Government Printing Office.

O'Beirne, Kate. "Girls with Guns." *National Review.* 49(13) 49-51.

O'Brien, Tim. 1999. *The Things They Carried: A Work of Fiction.* New York: Penguin Books.

Ohio Gun Collectors Association. 2008. "History of the Ohio Gun Collectors Association." Accessed on April 14, 2008 at http://www.ogca.com/History.htm.

Olmsted, A.D. 1988. "Morally Controversial Leisure: The Social World of Gun Collectors." *Symbolic Interaction*; 11:2, p277-287.

Olsen, Frances. 1990. "The Sex of Law." Pp 453-467 in *The Politics of Law A Progressive Critique, edited by David Kairey.* NY: Pantheon Books.

Pfuhl, Erdwin. 1986. *The Deviance Process.* (2nd ed.). Belmont, CA: Wadsworth.

Poudrier, Almira F. 2001. "The Virtue of the Weaponed Hero." *The Humanist.* July.

Pronger, B. 1990. "Gay Jocks: A Phenomenology of Gay Men in Athletics." Pp. 141-152 in *Sport, Men, and the Gender Order: Critical Feminist Perspectives, edited by* Michael Messner and Donald Sabo. Champaign, IL: Human Kinetics Books.

Prus, Robert. 1996. *Symbolic Interaction and Ethnographic Research.* Albany, NY: State University of New York Press.

Rosenblatt, Roger. 1999 "Get Rid of the Damned Things." *Time* 154:38-39.

Schaefer, Richard T. 2007. *Sociology: A Brief Introduction* (7th ed.). McGraw-Hill.

Schneider, Joseph W., and Peter Conrad. 1980. "In the Closet with Illness: Epilepsy, Stigma Potential and Information Control." *Social Problems* 28:32-44.

Schwartz, Emma. 2008. "Gun Control Laws." *U.S. News & World Report.* Accessed on June 14, 2008 at http://www.usnews.com/articles/news/politics/2008/03/06/gun-control-laws.html.

Scott, Marvin B. and Stanford M. Lyman. 1968. "Accounts." *American Sociological Review* 33: 46-62.

Segal, Lynne. 1990. *Slow Motion: Changing Masculinities, Changing Men.* New Brunswick, NJ: Rutgers University Press.

Seidman, Steven. 2004. *Contested Knowledge: Social Theory Today.* Malden, MA: Blackwell Publishing.

Single Action Shooting Society. 2008. *Shooters Handbook.* Accessed on April 14, 2008 at www.sassnet.com/Downloads/RO/SASSHandbook(14).pdf.

Shideler, Dan. 2008. *The Official Gun Digest Book of Guns & Prices.* Iola, WI: Krause Publications.

Snow, David A. 1979. "A Dramaturgical Analysis of Movement Accommodation: Building Idiosyncrasy Credit as a Movement Mobilization Strategy." *Symbolic Interaction* 2:23-44.

Snow, David A., and Leon Anderson. 1993. *Down on Their Luck: A Study of Homeless Street People.* Berkeley, CA: University of California Press.

Snow, David A., Robert D. Benford, and Leon Anderson. 1986. "Fieldwork Roles and Informational Yield: A Comparison of Alternative Settings and Roles." *Urban Life* 14:377-408.

Snow, David A., Calvin Morrill, and Leon Anderson. 2003. "Elaborating Analytic Ethnography: Linking Fieldwork and Theory." *Ethnography* 2:181-200.

Squires, Peter. 2000. *Gun Culture or Gun Control? Firearms, Violence and Society.* London: Routhledge.

Stenross, Barbara. 1994. "Aesthetes in the Marketplace: Collectors in the Gun Business." *Qualitative Sociology.* 17:1.

Sykes, Gresham M. and David Matza. 1957. "Techniques of Neutralization: A Theory of Delinquency." *American Sociological Review.* 22: 664-670.

Taylor, Jimmy D. 2009. *American Gun Culture: Collectors, Shows and the Story of the Gun.* El Paso: LFB Scholarly.

Thio, Alex, Jim D. Taylor and Martin D. Schwartz. 2012. *Deviant Behavior* (11th ed.). Boston: Pearson Publishing.

Thorne, Deborah, and Leon Anderson. 2006. "Managing the Stigma of Personal Bankruptcy." *Sociological Focus* 39:77-98.

Turner, Jonathan. 2000. *On The Origins of Human Emotions.* Standord, CA: Stanford University Press.

Vigorito, Anthony. 1998. "Marketing Masculinity: Gender Identity and Popular Magazines." Sex Roles 39:135-152.

Warren, Carol A. B. 1980. "Destigmatization of Identity: From Deviant to Charismatic." *Qualitative Sociology* 3:59-72.

War, Mark. 1992. "Altruistic Fear of Victimization in Households." *Social Science Quarterly* 73(4):723-736.

Watson, Jonathan. 2000. *Male Bodies: Health, Culture and Identity.* Buckingham and Philadelphia: Open University Press.

West, Candace and Don Zimmerman. 1987. "Doing Gender." *Gender and Society*, 1(2): 125-151.

Whiteley, Sheila. 1997. *Sexing the Groove: Popular Music and Gender.* New York: Routhledge.

Wright, James D., Peter H. Rossi and Kathleen Daly. 1983. Under the Gun: Weapons, Crime, and Violence in America. New York: Aldine.

Zimring, Franklin and Gordon Hawkins. 1987. *The Citizens Guide to Gun Control.* New York: Macmillan Publishing.

_____. 1997. *Crime is Not the Problem: Lethal Violence in America.* New York: Oxford.

Index